T0286816

Cambridge Elements ☰

Elements in Public Policy
edited by
M. Ramesh
National University of Singapore (NUS)
Michael Howlett
Simon Fraser University, British Columbia
Xun WU
Hong Kong University of Science and Technology
Judith Clifton
University of Cantabria
Eduardo Araral
National University of Singapore (NUS)

UNDERSTANDING ACCOUNTABILITY IN DEMOCRATIC GOVERNANCE

Yannis Papadopoulos
University of Lausanne

CAMBRIDGE
UNIVERSITY PRESS

Shaftesbury Road, Cambridge CB2 8EA, United Kingdom

One Liberty Plaza, 20th Floor, New York, NY 10006, USA

477 Williamstown Road, Port Melbourne, VIC 3207, Australia

314–321, 3rd Floor, Plot 3, Splendor Forum, Jasola District Centre,
New Delhi – 110025, India

103 Penang Road, #05–06/07, Visioncrest Commercial, Singapore 238467

Cambridge University Press is part of Cambridge University Press & Assessment,
a department of the University of Cambridge.

We share the University's mission to contribute to society through the pursuit of
education, learning and research at the highest international levels of excellence.

www.cambridge.org
Information on this title: www.cambridge.org/9781108978231

DOI: 10.1017/9781108973823

© Yannis Papadopoulos 2023

This work is in copyright. It is subject to statutory exceptions and to the provisions
of relevant licensing agreements; with the exception of the Creative Commons version
the link for which is provided below, no reproduction of any part of this work may take
place without the written permission of Cambridge University Press & Assessment.

An online version of this work is published at doi.org/10.1017/9781108973823 under
a Creative Commons Open Access license CC-BY-NC-ND 4.0 which permits re-use,
distribution and reproduction in any medium for non-commercial purposes providing
appropriate credit to the original work is given. You may not distribute derivative
works without permission. To view a copy of this license, visit https://creativecommons
.org/licenses/by-nc-nd/4.0

All versions of this work may contain content reproduced under license from third parties.

Permission to reproduce this third-party content must be obtained from these
third-parties directly.

When citing this work, please include a reference to the DOI 10.1017/9781108973823

First published 2023

A catalogue record for this publication is available from the British Library.

ISBN 978-1-108-97823-1 Paperback
ISSN 2398-4058 (online)
ISSN 2514-3565 (print)

Cambridge University Press & Assessment has no responsibility for the persistence
or accuracy of URLs for external or third-party internet websites referred to in this
publication and does not guarantee that any content on such websites is, or will
remain,accurate or appropriate.

Understanding Accountability in Democratic Governance

Elements in Public Policy

DOI: 10.1017/9781108973823
First published online: February 2023

Yannis Papadopoulos
University of Lausanne

Author for correspondence: Yannis Papadopoulos, ioannis.papadopoulos
@unil.ch

Abstract: This Element comprehensively scrutinizes the key issue of the accountability of policy-makers in democratic governance. The electoral punishment of the incumbents, parliamentary control of the government and sanctions in the case of administrative misconduct or negligence are the most visible manifestations of accountability in politics. However, the phenomenon is much more complex, and fully understanding such a multifaceted object requires bridging bodies of work that usually remain disjointed. This Element assesses the effectiveness of vertical accountability through elections and how interinstitutional accountability operates in checks-and-balances systems, along with the growing role of the courts. It evaluates how the accountability of the bureaucracy has been affected by managerial reforms and different governance transformations. It also scrutinizes to what extent mediatization and policy failure boost accountability, before zooming in on the feelings and reactions of those who are held accountable. This title is also available as Open Access on Cambridge Core.

Keywords: accountability, democracy, governance, policy-making, public policy

ISBNs: 9781108978231 (PB), 9781108973823 (OC)
ISSNs: 2398-4058 (online), 2514-3565 (print)

Contents

1 Introduction: An Interactionist View of Accountability   1

2 The Crucial Role of Competitive Elections in Democratic
Accountability   6

3 Deparliamentarization, Horizontal Accountability
and Judicialization   14

4 Governance Transformations and the Policy Role
of the Bureaucracy   21

5 Managing Accountability in Monitory Democracy   37

6 Perceptions Matter: Overloads and Felt Accountability   47

7 Conclusion: Core Messages   54

References   64

1 Introduction: An Interactionist View of Accountability

We hold each other accountable in many social spheres. Not only are accountability relations ubiquitous, but few people would say that account-ability is a bad thing. In politics, accountability appears to be a virtue that is essential to democratic government and provides the legitimacy necessary for good governance. Accountability is employed as a catchword and has become an 'ever-expanding' (Mulgan, 2000a) 'magic concept' (Pollitt and Hupe, 2011), which often remains nebulous despite its aura. In academic scholarship, normative concerns matter, too, but the emphasis is on the analytical and empirical aspects of accountability, not the idealization. This means that different degrees and kinds of accountability may be suitable for different purposes, and Bovens (2010) distinguishes among three main perspectives on accountability depending on the goals it serves. Accountability serves not only to ensure control over representatives and rule-makers in general (democratic perspective) but also to prevent abuses of power (constitutional perspective) and enhance performance (learning perspective). As accountability is a multidimensional concept, studying how it operates requires one to identify the following:[1]

- Who is accountable to whom: both the account-giver and the account-holder (also called the 'accountor' and the 'accountee', respectively) can be individuals or organized actors and institutions; individuals may incarnate collectives, as in the case of hierarchical accountability in which organizational leadership assumes responsibility for any problems due to systemic errors within the organization (ministerial responsibility to parliament is a subcase thereof), and organizations as collectives may be held accountable for malfunctions caused by individuals who are part of them, as in the case of corporate accountability;
- For what: Rock (2020: 79) basically distinguishes between fault and outcomes, but one may differentiate among responsiveness to voters' preferences, respect for role requirements and procedural norms (such as fairness, impartiality or proportionality), performance and goal achievement, management of public funds, the personal qualities (such as probity) of politicians and so on;
- How, that is, through what kind of processes and under what kind of ground rules, explicit or implicit standards: political (for elected officials), administrative/ managerial (for civil servants), legal/judicial (if compliance with rules is at stake) and so on;

---

[1] This is adapted from Mashaw's (2006: 118) six basic features of accountability regimes.

- Possibly with what kinds of consequences: sanctions and rewards of different kinds or a change in the course of action, all of them considered remedies to a conduct judged problematic (whatever the reasons), and being part of the choice architecture supposed to deter account-givers from behaving in an unsuitable way.

Accountability must be seen as a social mechanism of a relational, and frequently also of a communicative, nature that connects individual or collective policy actors to an audience (often called a 'forum' in specialized literature). This happens in deliberative – sometimes also bargaining – processes, which can be more or less conflictual, and possibly under the threat of sanctions by account-holders in case of estimated misconduct or poor performance by account-givers. Accountability is, therefore, intimately related to power: being able to hold someone accountable indicates a privileged position, and one is less vulnerable if one can escape accountability (Waldron, 2014: 3). However, depending on the purpose of accountability, the power dimension may not be prominent. For example, policy-makers may voluntarily provide accounts to stimulate feedback from their interlocutors with the goal of learning from the exchange and improving the epistemic quality of policy.

Even if the monitoring of actors by forums can be concomitant with actors' behaviour and even if policy-makers anticipate the accountability phase, accountability basically takes place *ex post*. As Olsen (2015: 425) put it, 'accountability involves establishing facts and assigning causality and responsibility, formulating and applying normative standards for assessing conduct and reasons given, and building and applying capabilities for sanctioning inappropriate conduct'. The accountability relationship is usually disaggregated into three major steps. (1) An actor complies with a formal, moral or practical obligation – a reason-giving requirement – to explain and justify their conduct to a forum by providing information about procedures, performance or outcomes (answerability). (2) A debate may ensue, and the forum can pose questions and pass judgement so that the relationship can have a dialogical component. (3) The actor may face positive or negative consequences depending on the forum's evaluation, and the actor's decisions may be corrected, either because this is mandated by the forum or because the actor becomes aware of such a need (enforceability).[2] There is no necessary covariation among these three facets of accountability, which means that account-giving may be more or less detailed, but this may not necessarily impact deliberation, which may be more or less sustained, or sanctions, which may be more or less threatening (Brandsma and Schillemans, 2013).

---

[2] Adapted from Bovens, Goodin and Schillemans (2014), among many other works by Mark Bovens, who is at the origin of the conceptual disaggregation of the accountability circuit.

It is obvious that accountability, as it develops in practice (*de facto*), does not always function as formally prescribed 'on paper' (*de jure*), and this applies to all sequences of the accountability process. An interactionist approach to accountability requires not just familiarity with formal accountability regimes, which 'are sometimes empty shells or window dressing' (Olsen, 2017: 19), but also with existing informal accountability webs and mechanisms. One needs to scrutinize if and how a forum contests an actor's decisions and challenges the actor's justifications, if and how the actor engages with that contestation and if and how the forum reacts to the actor's reaction (Maricut-Akbik, 2020). As we shall see, accountability forums endowed with significant formal oversight competences – such as parliamentary assemblies – may prove to be 'paper tigers' if they are not willing or able to do their monitoring job. Accountability mechanisms are then toothless, and the exercise of accountability risks becoming ritualistic. In contrast, forums that only informally perform an accountability role, such as the media, may ruin organizational reputations or politicians' careers, taking the role of 'prosecutors' (Rock, 2020: 63) who seek to trigger reactions from forums that do have a formal sanctioning capacity. The effective exercise of forums' monitoring role clearly necessitates resources such as time and expertise, and forums may need to coordinate to pool these resources. Typically, for example, voters have a direct sanctioning capacity but may be poorly informed; they need to rely on media input, a well-informed forum without any formal sanctioning power (Mechkova, Lührmann and Lindberg, 2019: 46–7). This is not to say that forums necessarily coordinate, forming a coherent system: the existence of 'multiple eyes' may lead to overlaps – both unnecessary redundancies and inconsistencies – and ultimately to excess or messy accountability.

With respect to political accountability, two main sources legitimize a forum to exercise its prerogatives. The first is when the forum is a 'principal' that has previously delegated (some of its) prerogatives to an agent, as highlighted by 'principal–agent' theory. Although the latter is closely linked to the democratic perspective on accountability, it is used more generally as a framework to study the relations of representation and delegation. Being in such a relationship, the agent is accountable to the principal, and accountability is thus based on 'constituent sovereignty' (Goodhart, 2011: 47) or, in other words, on 'ownership' (Bovens, Goodin and Schillemans, 2014: 5). Typical examples are the accountability of elected officials to their constituencies, ministers to parliament, members of the bureaucracy to political superiors, leaders of interest groups to the rank-and-file and so on. The second source is affectedness: those who are (deliberately or not) affected by the outcomes of political decisions can claim to exercise a legitimate stakeholder right and hold output producers accountable, even more so if the affected have not participated or have not been influential in the decision-making process.[3] It is important not to conflate both sources because those impacted by the wielding of power may not be the same population as those – if any – who have delegated their power.[4] However, with the exception of the intended target population, it may be difficult to define affectedness, as this implies agreement about complex causation processes.[5] For instance, those asserting that they suffer collateral damage from policies must prove that their situation has deteriorated because of those policies. As a result, claims of affectedness may compete and be disputed. Apart from these forms of political accountability, formal office holders may be held accountable by third parties such as courts, which must normally be impartial. Courts can decide to investigate on their own initiative or can do so following complaints, the second option confirming that the exercise of accountability entails interdependence between forums.

As accountability in politics has multiple facets, it needs to be studied from various angles and through different conceptual lenses. This Element does so by bridging bodies of work that are seldom associated: studies on voting behaviour, institutional relations, public policy and administration, political communication, social psychology and democratic theory. Furthermore, this Element scrutinizes how transformations of governance – such as evolving executive–legislative relations, the more assertive role of the judiciary and administrative reform, including the growth of policy networks and of independent agencies – or the changing context thereof (such as the mediatization of politics) affect accountability relations. However, due to space limits, a full treatment of such a multisided phenomenon as accountability is beyond the scope of this Element. By concentrating on the accountability of actors who produce or implement collectively binding decisions, this Element does not scrutinize the accountability of other categories of actors who, although they may be influential in the policy-making process,[6] are not officially mandated to issue authoritative

---

[3] This may raise the issue of ordinary citizens' responsibility as direct contributors to public decision-making, and whether they have any accountability duties in that role. Should we expect citizens to behave in a discursively defensible manner and to demonstrate public-mindedness when they make collectively binding decisions in elections and (even more so) in referendums? See the notion of 'internal-reflective deliberation' (Goodin, 2003) and the debates on vote secrecy (Vandamme, 2018).

[4] Emphasis on each of these sources is also related, to some extent, to different conceptions of democracy. While delegation issues are discussed within the classic framework of representative democracy, those related to stakeholder involvement usually denote a participatory approach. Even though deliberation occupies a central place in accountability processes, the latter are seldom studied by advocates of 'deliberative' democracy.

[5] For a thorough discussion, see Goodin (2007).

[6] There are many definitions of policy-making. The following is eloquent: 'policy-making is fundamentally about constrained actors attempting to match policy goals with policy means in

decisions and are not politically accountable. For instance, one may think of experts[7] whose advice and support may be necessary for efficient governmental action (think of public health specialists' roles in the management of the COVID-19 crisis) or journalists whose reports contribute to the public resonance of claims (think of the media's role in setting climate change on the agenda). Neither does this Element discuss how the wielding of power and the corresponding accountability scale up above the nation-state, although one should be aware of the limits of 'methodological nationalism' and acknowledge that policy-making often – and in all likelihood, increasingly – spans borders: it is shaped through and constrained by interactions between distinct jurisdictions and levels. Literature on the accountability of governance spheres beyond the nation-state is abundant, both regarding supranational systems such as the European Union and the many forms of policy-making at the global level.[8]

This Element is intended to provide a bird's eye view of accountability in systems of democratic governance[9] and is structured as follows for that purpose. Immediately after this introductory section, Section 2 conceptually disentangles how competitive elections operate as the core element of democratic accountability according to theories of representative democracy and then examines to what extent they effectively accomplish this crucial function. In addition, accountability relations between institutions are equally important, as suggested by the existence of checks and balances in democratic systems in which power is fragmented, and a special mention must be made of the increasing role of courts as accountability forums (Section 3). Section 4 focuses on further elements of the vertical delegation and accountability chain, between elected officials and appointed civil servants, within administrative hierarchies and in the increasingly complex and networked universe of state bureaucracies. Section 5 first zooms in on the watchdog role of the media in the context of

---

a process which can be characterized as "applied problem solving"' (Howlett, Ramesh and Perl, 2009: 4).

[7] See Langvatn and Holst (2022) for an illustration of normative and empirical problems related to experts' accountability.

[8] Apart from numerous journal articles, one can find a book-length treatment of accountability issues in the European Union by Bovens, Curtin and 't Hart (2010) on various European institutions, by Hobolt and Tilley (2014) on citizens' perspectives and by Markakis (2020) on the Economic and Monetary Union. Fabbrini's (2015) and Schmidt's (2020) works on European Union governance as a whole are very useful, too. For recent major contributions on accountability issues related to transnational governance spheres, one can refer to Grigorescu (2015) on the evolving accountability of intergovernmental organizations, Hirschmann (2020) on the United Nations system in the area of human rights, Montanaro (2017) on the role of NGOs as forums; see also Koenig-Archibugi (2017) for a synthesis.

[9] Accountability in autocratic regimes remains largely unexplored; the most notable exception is the burgeoning literature on Chinese public administration (see among other studies recently Wu and Christensen, 2021; Li, Qin and Koppenjan, 2022; Tu and Gong, 2022).

so-called audience democracy but also points out the limits of monitoring, including in crises. Finally, Section 6 digs into the subjective face of accountability to discuss the risks associated with potentially excessive pressure: how do individuals who experience control by accountability audiences perceive and react to it? The concluding section shows what makes accountability truly kaleidoscopic.

2 The Crucial Role of Competitive Elections in Democratic Accountability

Electoral accountability is an obvious precondition for representative government to be considered democratic. In what has been called the 'party government' approach to accountability (Sørensen, 2020: 59),[10] the existence of competitive elections in representative systems is considered the cornerstone of incumbents' democratic accountability and is, therefore, crucial for the responsiveness of their policies to citizens' preferences. This general (and positive) assessment first needs to be conceptually disentangled and then submitted to critical empirical scrutiny. This section first scrutinizes the mechanics of electoral accountability and emphasizes the crucial role of retrospective voting in that respect. The section then shows that the evidence is mixed regarding the effectiveness of that mechanism, which may be diminished due to voters' cognitive limitations and the fragmentation of power. Despite this, policies in established democracies seem by and large to match citizens' preferences. The section concludes that the sheer shadow of accountability may act as an incentive for office-holders in that respect, but the process leading to this reassuring observation remains a black box for students of electoral politics.

2.1 Accountability through Elections: The Pivotal Role of Retrospective Considerations

Before being a mechanism of *ex post* accountability that casts its shadow over decision-makers, elections are a mechanism of *ex ante* authorization to represent the people, which constitutes 'promissory' representation based on the prospective evaluation of pledges made by competing parties and candidates (Mansbridge, 2003). However, elections are a relatively crude instrument for the formulation of mandates, so we should not expect that the authorization to govern will necessarily determine the content of public policies. Despite the growing use of voting advice applications, we generally have relatively vague profiles of parties and candidates in mind and simply diffuse expectations from our representatives.

---

[10] See, apart from many classic studies, Maravall and Sanchez-Cuenca (2009).

Unsurprisingly, then, discretion is inherent to representative government, and principal–agent theory has convincingly demonstrated that delegation by a principal usually leads to the discretionary power of his or her agent (see Miller, 2005): if we apply the contractual metaphor to describe delegation mandates, apart from being implicit, the contract is an incomplete one, with many points remaining unspecified.[11] As a counterweight to the agents' discretionary power and related risk of opportunistic behaviour, principals need to hold them accountable to preserve their own interests. Therefore, in representative democracies, elections are also a mechanism of *ex post* accountability: the threat of electoral sanction should incentivize office-holders to keep their promises to voters so that citizens retain some of their self-determination despite their decision-making power being delegated.

To some extent, electoral accountability is condemnatory, with the importance of so-called negative voting that primarily seeks to punish 'rascals' by deauthorizing them to rule, a reflection of the more general prevalence of a negativity bias in politics (Soroka, 2014). However, the electoral sanction should primarily be seen as instrumental rather than purely expressive, and it is forward-looking in that it is intended to change the course of things even if voters have no clear prospective motives in mind.[12] Moreover, its sheer threat should act as a disciplinary device to discourage agents (representatives) from deviating from principals' (voters') preferences simply because it is rational for agents to anticipate in their calculations the future judgement of their principals and the potential consequences thereof (Manin, 1997: 179). For the effective operation of democratic government, the prospect of electoral accountability and sanction is most crucial, making the 'law of anticipated reactions' work (Friedrich, 1937). Absent this expectation – if incumbents discount the risk of being defeated in the next election, for example, in the absence of credible alternatives or because their electorate displays strong partisan loyalty – office-holders would have no incentives to remain responsive to the voters who selected them and temporarily authorized them to rule.

In such a democratic perspective on accountability, the latter serves as a mechanism regulating representative government through its 'thermostatic' action. This mechanism is designed to ensure the smooth coexistence of 'policy representation' and 'public responsiveness' (Soroka and Wlezien, 2010): to remain

---

[11] In the absence of imperative mandates in modern times, there is no explicit contract between voters and their representatives, but even in 'public service bargains' between politicians and administrators, matters related to competencies, responsibilities and rewards remain controversial (Hood and Lodge, 2006).

[12] The same happens in the case of horizontal accountability to 'veto' institutions, such as a second chamber or a court (see Section 3), which aims to amend or nullify policies that are not aligned with their preferences.

in power, governments are incentivized to adjust their policy choices to citizens' preferences,[13] and citizens in turn adjust their views to consider the existing supply of policies (the erosion of partisan identities and the prevalence of issue voting facilitating flexibility). In addition, representation is 'dynamic' (Stimson, Mackuen and Erikson, 1995): governments use policies to respond to perceived shifts in public opinion, and policies generate feedback effects, with voters also modifying their preferences depending on the changes they discern in governmental action and the outcomes thereof.

It is therefore important for democratic control that the electorate votes based on retrospective rather than just prospective considerations. For example, the evaluation of past performance in office provides useful information to assess the credibility of commitments concerning future performance. To what extent are voters motivated above all by their desire to evaluate the incumbent government, and is their retrospective assignation of responsibilities and evaluation of performance based on sound evidence? Research focusing essentially on economic voting – initially in the United States, and then with a comparative approach (Anderson, 2007; Duch and Stevenson, 2008) – established that, whether voters are concerned with their individual well-being (egocentric voting) or with the state of the economy of their country as a whole (sociotropic voting), they do reward or sanction governments depending on their evaluations. However, empirical research also suggests that voters encounter cognitive limitations in their appreciation. Voters' decisions are the outcome of complex cognitive processes: they are not just contingent on the evaluation of outcomes that voters attribute to policy; they also require that voters judge the responsibility of governments for these outcomes, their skills and their efforts (Hobolt and Tilley, 2014: 123). The necessary copresence of these elements renders the accountability chain fragile[14] and subject to bias, especially due to media coverage that can be misleadingly negative (Achen and Bartels, 2017: 108).

2.2 Evidence on Voting Patterns: A Mixed Picture

Findings from survey and experimental research indicate that people use short-cuts to make their decisions on political matters: heuristics, such as party cues,

---

[13] Note that this can also be criticized as 'electoralism' and associated with short-termism. Responsiveness to voters may create the wrong incentives for decision-makers, so that in some cases, insulation from voters may be preferable. This is a major justification for the diffusion of the independent agency phenomenon (see Section 4). On hurdles to future-oriented policy-making and difficulties in trading short-term costs for long-term gains, see Jacobs (2011).

[14] According to de Vries and Solaz (2017), to punish incumbents for corruption, voters need to go through the stages of information acquisition, blame attribution and behavioural response (switching, abstaining or sticking to their previous vote). If one or more of these stages breaks down, punishment may not happen.

the opinions of friends, media frames or the positions of interest groups, are useful in that respect, and even more so for those (generally those who are less educated) who lack familiarity with politics. They thereby reduce upper-class bias in participation in public affairs, but this may lead to inadequate conclusions and poorly informed choices. Shortcuts are instrumental in overcoming informational shortfalls and making decisions despite the complexity of political matters but do not protect against evaluation and attribution errors due to bounded rationality (such as overemphasizing recent events or overweighting incumbents' broken pledges).

Achen and Bartels (2017) challenged what they call the 'romantic folk theory' of democracy, according to which voters would choose parties and candidates on the basis of genuine evaluations of policy. They demonstrated that voters' choices continue to be tainted by social identities and partisan loyalties, with ideology being an information-saving device used as a filter to decode reality. Ideology thus allows voters to surmount cognitive limits to some extent, considering that the retrospective model sets the bar too high with respect to the level of sophistication required from voters. However, as preexisting views of the world serve as perceptual screens, responsibility judgements are biased by prior political beliefs: 'people prefer to give credit for good outcomes to political actors they already like and are equally willing to blame poor outcomes on political actors they already dislike' (Hobolt and Tilley, 2014: 49). For example, partisanship colours perceptions of the economic situation and of who is responsible for the good or bad state of the economy (see, among many others, Tilley and Hobolt, 2011). Furthermore, voters exaggerate politicians' influence (Caplan et al., 2013), and irrelevant events seem to affect evaluations of governmental performance.

Healy, Malhotra and Mo (2010) explore the electoral impact of local college football games in the United States just before an election, assuming that people often transfer emotions in one domain towards judgement in a different domain. Obviously, football games are completely unrelated to public affairs and governmental actions. Nonetheless, the authors find that a win in the ten days before Election Day caused the incumbent party to (marginally) increase its vote in the Senate, gubernatorial and presidential elections between 1964 and 2008, with the effect being larger for teams with stronger fan support. They conclude by noting 'the subtle power of irrelevant events in shaping important real-world decisions'.

However, there are also more optimistic views. Debating the assumption that the government is commonly blamed for people's misfortune, even if it is not responsible for 'bad times' such as floods or droughts, Gasper and Reeves (2011) showed that the electorate is able to separate random events such as natural accidents from governmental responses. Using various counterexamples, Stokes (2018) concluded that Achen and Bartels' severe judgement needs to be nuanced. Some citizens are more predisposed than others to tame affect and partisanship with reflection (Arceneaux and Vander Wielen, 2017). For example, evaluating the inadequate governmental response to Hurricane Katrina, more sophisticated respondents to a survey in Louisiana were less prone to focus blame disproportionately on the president as the most obvious national political figure (Gomez and Wilson, 2008).[15] Findings from a study based on data from twenty-five democracies across an array of policy areas, including the economy, social welfare, immigration and national security, confirm that holding governments accountable for past performance is mainly the prerogative of highly sophisticated citizens (de Vries and Giger, 2014). At the same time, however, the sophistication gap narrows when voters attach a higher degree of salience to a policy area, that is, when the issues at stake are important to them. After all, isn't that what counts most for electoral accountability?

2.3 Systemic Variables Matter

The effectiveness of electoral accountability also depends on the institutional architecture of the political system. An analysis of elections from seventy-five countries revealed that separation-of-powers systems are superior in terms of accountability; however, this is only true under the condition of strong party competition and with the exceptions of semipresidentialism and episodes of cohabitation (Hellwig and Samuels, 2008). The reward–punishment model works best when the mechanisms of accountability are simple (Anderson, 2000), which is not surprising if we think of the sophistication required to allocate responsibility and evaluate performance. Blurring responsibility and strengthening cognitive bias, vertical and horizontal institutional and power fragmentation attenuate democratic accountability and the effect of evaluations on incumbents' popularity.

Such structural features are considered to negatively impact electoral accountability in federalist political systems in which policies are produced at various jurisdictional levels. Federalism allows for opportunities to designate representatives at multiple levels but complicates effective popular control by

---

[15] In line with attitudinal research on the personification of the state (McGraw and Dolan, 2007).

generating confusion about who is in charge of policies (León, 2018). Lack of clarity concerning responsibility facilitates adherence to the blame-shifting frames produced by political elites to evade responsibility for poor performance, as in the case of the responses to Hurricane Katrina.

Maestas et al. (2008) study the effects of the strategies deployed by national, state and local government officials to shift blame for the poor response to Hurricane Katrina to other levels of government. The authors show that attempts by national political actors to blame the state government of Louisiana were successful, but the size of the effect was conditional on predispositions. Individuals who rated themselves as conservatives or Republicans were more likely to blame the Democratic state government for failing to call for enough help. Those who were more attentive to media coverage patterns were also more likely to believe the state's failure to call for help was to blame for the length of time it took for the national government to provide aid to New Orleans.

Using data from the European Election Studies, León, Jurado and Madariaga (2018) found that when partisans of the national government in federal states are confronted with poor economic outcomes, they are more likely to 'pass the buck' to the regional level following a blame-shift logic, while this mechanism is absent in non-federal states. Cutler (2008) concluded that federalism is challenging for Canadian voters wishing to reward or punish their governments for policy outcomes. They do not easily distinguish the roles of different jurisdictional levels, and there is little variation across issues; attentiveness to politics only very slightly improves the quality of responsibility attributions and only on issues where responsibility is objectively clearer. A recent study showed that interprovincial policy variation with respect to coronavirus testing in Canada is not correlated with public assessments of the adequacy of provincial testing, confirming that Canadians have difficulty assigning responsibility to the correct level of government despite high levels of issue saliency and media attention (Kennedy, Sayers and Alcantara, 2022).

These studies all concur that multilevel structures risk undermining responsibility attribution and thus democratic accountability, and we should keep in mind that the complexity of multilevel arrangements usually goes far beyond the formal distribution of power. Competences are not just divided between jurisdictional levels; they are also frequently shared among them, and different levels may need to pool resources to make policies. All this necessitates collaboration between multiple interdependent actors entangled in dense networks with informal interactions that are not easily visible from the outside. In other words, even if citizens are able to allocate formal responsibilities correctly, they may only see the most visible part of the actual policy-making processes, with a possible gap between accountability and the wielding of power (see Section 4).

Moreover, the characteristics of the party system mediate the role of elections as an accountability mechanism. Proportional representation secures a fairer and more pluralist representation of political forces but risks leading to excessive fragmentation of the party system and to a multiparty government that dilutes responsibility. In contrast, first-past-the-post electoral systems set high thresholds for representation but facilitate the formation of single-party governments. They also tend to induce bipolar dynamics, which makes it easier to identify clear alternatives that deserve to be supported. A recent comparative analysis with data from 400 parliamentary elections (Kam, Bertelli and Held, 2020) revealed that electoral gains and losses are more clearly mirrored in the gains and losses of ministerial portfolios in strongly bipolar party systems, while multiparty systems increase the risk of unstable majorities, with the consequence that losers in elections may remain in office. Furthermore, experimental evidence suggests that legislators elected in single-member constituencies have more sustained interactions with their voters and are more reactive to the requests of this particular – admittedly narrow – segment of the electorate (constituency service) (Breunig, Grossman and Hänni, 2022).

Allocating responsibility may be even more difficult when the government is divided, as in presidential systems with different majorities in the executive and the legislative resulting in a relatively weak government facing a strong 'veto point', or when the legislature is bicameral, with two differently composed chambers. However, it seems that the cohesiveness of the national government is the key factor (Hobolt, Tilley and Banducci, 2013): government becomes a clearly identifiable target, and according to survey data from twenty-seven European countries, this matters most for clarity of responsibility, regardless of whether institutional power is shared (in upper chambers, other levels of government, etc.).[16] This is reassuring because it appears that institutional checks can tame majoritarian discretion without greatly hampering democratic accountability.

2.4 Policy Responsiveness: The Invisible Hand?

Equally reassuring from the democratic perspective on accountability is the fact that public opinion indeed operates as a 'thermostat' despite the limits of retrospective voting. This is likely because governments fear voters' discontent

---

[16] This goes partially in the direction of Royed, Leyden and Borrelli (2000: 677–80), who found that the crucial variable is single-party as opposed to coalition government and criticized the widely cited clarity of responsibility index by Powell and Whitten (1993: 398–403), which included more variables mattering for clarity of responsibility.

and usually care about the risk of sanctions, even if voters are not always well equipped to evaluate governments' actions. Popular control of the government may rely on misperceptions, and elections are not an optimal instrument of accountability due both to issue bundling (governments simultaneously conduct multiple policies on which they can be evaluated) and the difficulties of comparing actual governmental performance with the more or less credible pledges of challengers. However, governments apprehend democratic control simply because it would be too risky for them to bet on its weaknesses. The degree of congruence between opinion preferences and policy is indeed remarkable (Rasmussen, Reher and Toshkov, 2019). In return, governmental parties are more likely to be rewarded by voters if they have fulfilled more of their pledges during incumbency (Matthieß, 2020).

> Rasmussen, Reher and Toshkov (2019) study the link between public opinion and policy, covering many issues in thirty-one European democracies with diverse institutional structures. They find a high level of congruence between the preferences of the majority and the content of policy, especially when the policy issue is highly salient in the media. Important differences exist across issues, but policy is more likely to reflect the opinion of the majority when the majority is large, in line with a correlation between the likelihood of policy being enacted and the degree of support.

Of course, this virtuous circle is welcome from a democratic perspective on representation. However, the main limitation of the studies that conclude with such positive results is that the processes leading to the congruence between governments and public opinion are not scrutinized in depth (de Wilde and Rauh, 2019). Policy-making remains a black box, and it is unclear what kinds of tools decision-makers use to recognize the signals emerging from public opinion (or from narrower but more easily identifiable electoral clienteles) and to influence political demand. Research on politicians' perceptions and strategic moves would also benefit from empirical findings on reputation management by senior staff in public agencies and social psychological research on how individuals experience accountability pressure (see Sections 4 and 6, respectively).

Furthermore, unpacking the black box often reveals actors other than authoritative government officials who influence the course of things without being held politically accountable: think of the roles of experts, interest group representatives or even editorialists. A conception of democratic regimes that focuses on the citizens–elections–representatives triad is no doubt normatively attractive due to the direct line that it posits upwards from 'we the people' to the government and downwards from the government to society (Hupe and Edwards, 2012: 182).

However, this conception does not adequately capture the way the governmental process works, as the next sections will show.

3 Deparliamentarization, Horizontal Accountability and Judicialization

In parliamentary systems of government, legislatures can be seen as the principals and governments as their agents, this being the next element of the delegation chain after the voters, as the ultimate principals, have delegated their decision-making power to legislators. In that sense, ministerial accountability to the legislature is an element of the vertical accountability chain that runs in the reverse direction of the delegation chain, with accountability of the public administration to its political superiors being the next element in the chain (see Section 4). Checks that impose restraints with the goal of avoiding abuses of power and, more generally, control of an institution by other institutions in the same political system that is grounded on the doctrine of separation of powers are commonly included in the category of horizontal accountability.[17] In other words, accountability relations are considered horizontal when they involve formal institutions endowed with relatively equal power. This section addresses both legislative–executive relations and horizontal accountability, with an emphasis on the growing role of courts as forums.

3.1 Checks and Balances: A Composite Image

The capacity of legislators to oversee governmental activity effectively depends on a wide range of factors (Pelizzo and Stapenhurst, 2014). The institutional setting matters, of course. Taking the case of the United Kingdom's model of 'Westminster'-style parliamentarism, the formal accountability chain is simple, with a direct line that has the merit of clarity from government to parliament and from parliament to the electorate. However, this model leaves little space for effective horizontal checks, as power is concentrated in the cabinet or even in the hands of the prime minister, and the governing party usually controls a disciplined majority in parliament. The opposition may 'bark' as expected in a logic of adversarial partisan politics but is not able to 'bite' (Wright, 2015). More specific factors also matter; for example, cross-country research suggests that the control of parliamentary committee chairs significantly strengthens opposition parties' ability to engage in legislative review (Fortunato, Martin and Vanberg, 2019). In non-parliamentary systems, as in the United States' presidential government, the executive becomes dominant (Posner and Vermeule, 2011), but it undergoes

---

[17] O'Donnell (1998) initially applied the concept to political systems in Latin America, where he deplored the atrophy of horizontal accountability.

significant pressure in its horizontal accountability obligations towards the legislature, despite its powers (Kriner and Schickler, 2017). Particularly in situations of 'divided government' in which different parties control the presidency and Congress, the existence of a regime of power separation incentivizes each branch to be sensitive to the preferences of the other branch. This prompts formal or informal interbranch bargaining to avoid policy blockades, but it is difficult to avoid the latter when partisan polarization is strong.

Notwithstanding cross-country differences, the recent transformations of governance styles challenge parliaments' power and seem to be at the origin of a more or less pronounced 'deparliamentarization'. In the next section, we will assess the consequences of the fragmentation of power with the advent of collaborative and delegated modes of governance. A competing narrative emphasizes the rampant concentration of power with the 'presidentialization' of politics (Poguntke and Webb, 2005) and the advent of 'court government' (Savoie, 2008), dominated by the prime minister, who is surrounded by an informal group of her or his few favourite ministers, and expert staff of policy professionals, public servants and PR specialists (Svallfors, 2020). Whatever the most accurate narrative of governance transformations, both the fragmentation of power in polycentric networks of actors and its concentration in the hands of the executive are considered to negatively impact parliamentary influence. In addition, the general trends of the last decades, such as the increased complexity of policy matters or the internationalization of policy-making, have lessened the centrality of legislative bodies in law-making processes and reduced their roles as accountability forums that hold governments – and rule-making entities more generally – accountable.

With policy issues requiring considerable expertise and policy-making moving partly into less visible negotiation arenas (sometimes even beyond the national state), parliaments are confronted with situations of information asymmetry, to their detriment. Moreover, parliamentarians may not just be unprepared to check executives; they may be unwilling to do so, as with members of governmental parties, or when the issues at stake are of low salience to them and not generating any electoral payoffs. Some parliaments have nevertheless reacted to their loss of power and managed to 'fight back' (Raunio and Hix, 2000), as with the development of parliamentary Select Committees in the United Kingdom, which scrutinize, conduct inquiries and report on governmental work (Schonhardt-Bailey, 2022). However, the strength of parliamentary reactions varies (Auel, Rozenberg and Tacea, 2015), and perhaps more importantly, even this countertrend generates trade-offs with regard to accountability because the parliamentary scrutiny of governmental work is most effective when exercised informally. This is detrimental to the external accountability to the general public, especially as parliamentary control power translates into influence and bargaining that develop in secluded arenas (Auel and Benz, 2005). Informality and lack of transparency aggravate citizens' difficulty in allocating responsibility (see Section 2).

Unlike democratic accountability to voters, horizontal accountability between institutions mirrors the constitutional perspective on accountability as a mechanism curtailing abuses of power by establishing checks on rulers' authority. The primary tool in that respect is the possibility to veto decisions, and the more veto points a political system contains (Immergut, 1992), the more rule-makers become accountable to veto 'players' (Tsebelis, 2003), that is, actors able to block or turn down decisions that do not match their preferences. In the case of symmetric bicameralism, for example – with two legislative chambers endowed with equal competences on important matters – the support of legislation by both chambers is necessary. To avoid the deadlock arising from disagreement between the two houses and the exercise of mutual veto rights, conference committees are set up in which deliberation and informal bargaining take place. Although this is not formulated as such in the literature on veto points, each side becomes *de facto* accountable to the other in these arenas, as it needs to convince the other side about its preferences. Moreover, when policy-makers face such an incentive structure that induces self-restraint and mutual adjustment, they are likely to anticipate and incorporate the expectations of veto players who act as *de facto* accountability forums. In other words, they are incentivized to absorb forums' preferences and objections even before these forums formulate any feedback.[18]

Findings from research on four decades of German bicameralism confirm that the shadow of veto power acts as a *de facto* super-majority requirement and thus fosters cooperative behaviour. If the opposition controls a majority in the second chamber that enjoys veto power, this leads to a more consensual relationship between government and opposition parties. Both sides, then, seek compromises early in the legislative process, and they are much more likely to vote the same way in parliament to avoid bicameral conflicts (Hohendorf, Saalfeld and Sieberer, 2021).

A more recent phenomenon is the growing horizontal accountability of rule-makers to institutions with a core oversight function,[19] which draw

---

[18] According to the law of anticipated reactions (see Section 2).

[19] Bovens and Wille (2021) distinguish between 'watchdog' institutions (such as auditing offices and anti-corruption agencies) with oversight as their only task, and oversight by less specialized institutions that perform other tasks as well, such as courts.

their legitimacy from being independent and non-majoritarian. Their mission is to safeguard the rule of law and protect minorities and individuals from violations of their rights and, more generally, to ensure compliance with principles of good governance. Traditionally, courts are the relevant forums for legal accountability, but auditing institutions have gained importance as forums of financial accountability with the movement towards performance evaluation and measurement (see Section 4). It is also worth noting that the hard accountability of public authorities to this kind of body, with assorted sanctions, is currently frequently accompanied by softer forms of account-ability. A prominent example is accountability to ombudsman institutions: although the latter have no direct sanctioning power, they can mandate public organizations to justify their decisions and practices. It is sometimes remarked that ombudsman institutions' lack of a formal 'bite' can be offset through creative operation (for instance, with an active communication policy) that pressures public authorities to comply (Bovens and Wille, 2021: 859–60). This would be potentially a case of an oversight institution whose *de facto* power to control and impose a change of practice is greater than the institution's *de jure* prerogatives.

3.2 Judicial Activism: Janus-Faced

The remainder of this section is dedicated to the power that the judiciary draws from its growing role as an accountability forum, which resulted from concerns about the risk of tyranny by the majority and more generally of abuses of power by rulers but also out of the strategic calculations of institutional designers (Vanberg, 2015). In recent decades, courts have seen their role gaining import-ance, especially regarding their capacity to overrule legislation considered incom-patible with constitutional or human rights principles. The emergence of a 'transnational legal order' (Shaffer, Ginsburg and Halliday, 2019) embodied in the 'global spread of constitutional review' (Ginsburg, 2008) has paralleled the successive waves of democratization, mostly in Europe and Latin America. As forums to which rule-makers are accountable, courts intrude into the policy-making process in response to complaints or on their own initiative, depending on the judicial system.[20] Judicial activism is a dimension of the broader 'rise of the unelected' (Vibert, 2007) that is also visible in the diffusion of the agency phenomenon (see Section 4).

---

[20] The phenomenon is also observable beyond the nation-state, such as in European countries with the role of the Court of Justice of the European Union and, beyond the EU, with the role of the European Court of Human Rights (an institution of the Council of Europe). On the varying influence of international courts around the globe on domestic legal and political orders, see Alter, Helfer and Madsen (2018).

The judiciary draws its legitimacy as an accountability forum from its independence, which is nevertheless subject to empirical variation and sometimes the object of political controversy. The so-called judicialization of politics first means that courts become policy actors just by being asked to arbitrate policy controversies, even if they do not aim to advance any particular policy preferences. Beyond that, judicialization is prompted by constitutionalization: judges become *de facto* co-legislators when courts possess constitutional review rights because legislators are then incentivized to anticipate their verdict. By acting as veto players capable of striking down legislation (regardless of their motivations), courts become pivotal actors and indirectly take over legislative functions. Like the shadow of future elections that incentivizes incumbents to be responsive to voters' preferences, the shadow of court rulings perceived as likely to reverse legislation prompts elected officials to absorb the preferences attributed to the judiciary. In the United States, for example, a newer area of interbranch bargaining research incorporates the judicial branch into the model of separation of powers: legislators seek to reach decisions that are as close as possible to their own preferences but robust to court interference (Knight and Schwartzberg, 2020: 268).

Moreover, although courts are primarily considered 'negative' legislators because of their formal veto rights, which allow them to nullify legislation, they may actually be more than that. They make recommendations in their rulings as to how legal acts should be revised, and the official legislators subsequently tend to follow them *ex post* in addition to being incentivized to take judges' anticipated opinions into account *ex ante*. Needless to say, when judges' preferences conflict with voters' preferences, elected officials may be caught in accountability dilemmas. These dilemmas are reflected in the debates on judicialization within political philosophy and legal theory, as Wright (2015: 100) observes: 'While political constitutionalism asserts the primacy of democratic politics as the arena of accountability and the necessary limitations of the role of unelected judges, legal constitutionalism points to the dangers of mere majoritarianism and the need for the protective accountabilities that only an independent judiciary can provide.'

The frictions between the exercise of popular or parliamentary sovereignty embodied in majority rule and the protection of individual and minority rights guaranteed by the rule of law as interpreted by courts have given rise to controversies regarding the quality of democracy. Developments in the direction of judicialization are welcomed by those defending a liberal–constitutionalist conception of democracy, who set the rule of law and protection of rights as primary objectives and criticize 'defective democracies' (Merkel, 2004) for not providing sufficient countervailing powers to unrestrained majority rule.

This approach builds on the fact that, when courts are perceived as independent and impartial, they usually enjoy strong legitimacy. Courts as institutions and judges as professionals tend to build credit and consolidate their reputations in the long run (as independent agencies and their expert staff do, as described in Section 4). They usually enjoy high levels of positive opinions from the general public, although – or maybe rather because[21] – they constrain popularly elected policy-makers (Garoupa and Ginsburg, 2015). Therefore, legal constitutionalism praises courts' contribution to good governance when they act as safeguards against democratic backsliding (Blauberger and Kelemen, 2017), when the judiciary is seen as a favourable venue for the development of rights (Cichowski, 2013), or when a growing number of international courts act as norm entrepreneurs to strengthen the rule of law and promote democratic practice, including holding states (as well as transnational actors) accountable and inducing them to provide public justifications (Kuyper and Squatrito, 2017). Obviously, this doctrine is highly critical of situations in which governmental interference undermines the independence of justice, as it recently happened in European Union member states such as Hungary and Poland.

In contrast, critics contend that the rule of law entails the 'rule of lawyers' (Kratochwil, 2008). Those who do not feel comfortable with the consequences of judicialization point out the 'counter-majoritarian difficulty' that is inherent to it – in other words, the risk that majority rule is undermined by judicial activism. They are worried about the risk of the formal separation of powers being undermined, but more than that, they criticize the advent of government by judges, who are politically unaccountable by design (as a condition of their independence) and most likely unrepresentative. To what extent should unelected accountability forums be able – in the name of impartiality and the public interest – to hold elected politicians accountable and indirectly incentivize elected officials to consider their views? This is an open question, but it can only be answered in light of the evidence regarding the amplitude of judicialization, which is admittedly mixed.

On the one hand, judicialization affects the treatment of 'mega' issues such as the importance of secularism, the contours of citizenship and national identity, electoral legislation and outcomes, corruption indictments and impeachment, bans on political parties and, more generally, the shaping of the democratic process itself as in rulings about transitional justice or emergency legislation (Hirschl, 2008). Although many of these issues speak to the core of the polity as such, reflect deeply salient dilemmas and ought to be the object of deliberation

---

[21] Just as the impartiality of independent agencies may be preferred over rule-making by elected politicians deemed vulnerable to capture by special interests (see Section 4).

in the public sphere, they have recently been framed in several countries as constitutional issues. As political authorities are unwilling or unable to resolve them, they transfer the problem to the judicial circuit; but judicial intervention can also take place unsolicited. Whatever its origin, such a process of depoliticization leading to a 'juristocracy' is normatively problematic, especially if one also considers the spread of quasi-constitutional supranational treaties and legal institutions that place several facets of global governance beyond democratic reach (Hirschl, 2013).

The global nature of the trend described by Hirschl should indeed not be underestimated: 'Please fasten your seatbelts', wrote the author before enumerating a long list of high-profile cases that illustrate his argument. However, in large part, the trend affects polities that face deadlock or weakly consolidated democracies, sometimes with a politicized judiciary that is instrumentalized by political forces. There is also contrasting evidence, which should rather lead us to conclude that the claims about the rising influence of non-democratically legitimized judges are overstated. Despite judges enjoying discretion, governments can adopt court-curbing measures, implement court rulings selectively (if not ignore or even override them) and ultimately seek to strip courts of their power.

Backlash may be difficult if the constitution must be amended for that purpose and costly if courts enjoy public support, but judicial power is not unrestrained even in well-established constitutional democracies: a comparative study of the United States, France and Germany covering thirty-six years (1974 to 2009) showed that the ability of constitutional courts to act as veto players is subject not just to cross-country but also to temporal variation because it depends on the way judges are selected, the pattern of government control, the rhythm of governmental alternation and the type of legislative procedures (Brouard and Hönnige, 2017). Moreover, judicial review can also directly or indirectly contribute to policy-makers' goals, so that an influential judiciary is not necessarily 'a nuisance that a dominant coalition would want to eliminate' (Vanberg, 2015: 172). Judges are sensitive (and perhaps even adhere) to the preferences of the majority of public opinion, and even independent judges care about policy-makers' preferences and feel restrained by the shadow of court packing measures, just as policy-makers care about and seek to anticipate judges' opinions. In sum, the relationship between the political and judicial spheres is one of an interplay between actors that are interdependent and behave strategically under this kind of constraint.

Overall, decision-makers in established democracies experience different kinds of horizontal accountability constraints. Empirically, it is difficult to observe a clear-cut trend; cross-country variation remains important, and there are developments that hamper interinstitutional accountability. Regarding the normative evaluation of horizontal accountability, the complexity of our societies may justify the existence of multiple checks on power wielders, and horizontal mechanisms are considered more likely to constrain governmental choices than vertical accountability to voters because institutional forums have the capacity to directly oversee governments continuously and apply direct sanctions. At the same time, for horizontal accountability to operate properly, it must be coupled with vertical accountability to citizens and effective societal accountability, regardless of frictions arising between these accountability forms: as Mechkova, Lührmann and Lindberg (2019: 58) observed, 'Without fully clean elections, autonomous opposition parties and a developed civil society and media, no country in the world has yet achieved fully effective government oversight through independent high courts, vigorous parliaments, or other institutions'.

Ultimately, with more assertive parliaments and with judicialization, executive and administrative power wielders become more accountable to other – elected or unelected – elites: politicians and judges. These interinstitutional modes of accountability may mitigate accountability to the citizenry by design, but they may also undermine it unintentionally. As we shall see in the next section, similar questions can be raised about the accountability of the bureaucracy after numerous administrative reforms.

4 Governance Transformations and the Policy Role of the Bureaucracy

The bureaucracy is the natural extension of the cabinet in the chain of delegation, and it is a policy-maker in its own right (Huber and Shipan, 2002; Potter, 2019; Rudalevige, 2021). Many studies have demonstrated the roles of groups of top civil servants as 'programmatic elites' with clear views of the policy reforms that they believe must be carried out (Hassenteufel and Genieys, 2021) or of individual bureaucrats as policy 'brokers' who mediate between opposing coalitions and are active in the pursuit of compromise (Ingold and Varone, 2012).

While students of politics are not usually very concerned about the components of the accountability chain beyond voters and elected officials, research by public administration specialists on the corporate accountability of administrative units and the individual accountability of civil servants covers the whole administrative hierarchy: from 'mandarins' at the top to mid-level managers and professionals and down to the street level. It is assumed that an accountability chain runs parallel to but in the reverse direction of the delegation chain (Strom, 2000): in an administrative hierarchy, principals not only delegate missions to lower-level agents but also do so with control, as top-level civil servants entrust mid-level staff with the oversight of frontline workers. However, contemporary governance architecture and practice complicate both delegation and accountability relations. Suffice it to say that holding organizations accountable is much more challenging than holding individuals accountable (Peters, 2014: 213). Therefore, it is convenient but can also be misleading to hold organizational leadership responsible for the systemic errors of their organizations. This section delves into the intricacies of the evolving mechanisms of administrative accountability.

It does so by first briefly pointing out the limits, trade-offs and side effects of the exercise of political control over the bureaucracy. It then highlights the major changes in accountability relations that originate in successive waves of administrative reform across countries. Namely, these changes include the shift to performance accountability that is supposed to move 'downwards' to societal forums, the proliferation of network forms of governance and the outsourcing or 'coproduction' of public services and the delegation of tasks to agencies that operate at arm's length from the government.

4.1 Delegation and the Limits of Political Control over the Bureaucracy

For those adhering to the principal–agent model of delegation, accountability is an essential element of the incentive structure that predisposes agents to act in accordance with their principals' preferences. The model emphasizes the risk of moral hazard by assuming that agents are motivated by the pursuit of self-interest, but the disconnect from the preferences of elected officials may simply be because the administration has its own conceptions of good policy (Peters, 2014: 211). Hence, for different reasons, elected officials may find that control of the bureaucracy is necessary, but they may also be inconvenienced by it: control necessitates time investments for acquiring expertise and energy in conducting scrutiny, which in turn entails opportunity costs. Is there any functional equivalent?

'Stewardship theory' presents itself as an alternative to principal–agent theory: it challenges its narrow economistic assumptions,[22] and it is grounded by contrast on a psychological understanding of actors' orientations and on a sociological understanding of the organizational context of action. Its advocates find that agency theory is too cynical and believe that agents behave as

---

[22] Another limit of the principal–agent model is its limited applicability to unsettled political orders in which the division of roles between principals and agents is challenged, and delegation mandates and provisions for accountability contested (Christensen and Lægreid, 2017; Olsen, 2017).

'stewards' who deserve to be trusted, as they are animated by a feeling of duty and find their self-realization in behaviour that is collective-minded and oriented towards the attainment of organizational goals (Davis, Schoorman and Donaldson, 1997).[23] To be sure, this trust may be misplaced, but agency drift can be mitigated if agents display strong value commitments, if they are socialized in the values of their principals, or if they adhere to the norm that their principals – whatever their values – have the authority to command. Scrutiny and sanctions then become unnecessary (and even potentially demotivating), as the agent feels that obeying the principal is the right (or normal) thing to do. To use March and Olsen's (2013) distinction, compliance is not obtained through a logic of consequences, that is, with the anticipation of rewards and sanctions, but through a logic of appropriateness: it is rule-based and, as such, is normatively valued conduct.

However, the stewardship model is excessively optimistic. Although a sense of responsibility is necessary, internal checks may not suffice without external control, for instance, to prevent or correct errors by loyal servants. However, we also need to be aware of the structural limitations of control due to the length of the delegation and accountability chains, combined with the uncertainty that affects processes in each of their parts. In Max Weber's traditional conception of bureaucracy, hierarchy plays a crucial role in ensuring compliance, but even low-level frontline professionals enjoy relative autonomy from their superiors because, for example, they can dissimulate information from them. In addition, as they are embedded in webs of informal relations, they may face incompatible expectations, standards and prescriptions for action from their superiors upwards, target groups, service users and regulatees downwards, and their professional peers sideways (Hupe and Hill, 2007; Romzek et al., 2014).

Of course, deliberate overlaps may enhance the robustness of an accountability regime. There are more opportunities to call to account, the functioning of accountability no longer depends on a single forum, and individual flaws can be compensated for by duplication (Willems and Van Dooren, 2012). However, if multiple demands and steering signals are uncoordinated, this may expand the

---

[23] These contrasting approaches resonate by and large with the debate between Herman Finer and Carl Friedrich in the beginning of the 1940s. Finer (1941) advocated a clear demarcation between politics and the administration as well as a hierarchical chain of command and accountability assorted with sanctions. Friedrich (1940), in contrast, considered such a model ill-suited to cope with the complexities of policy-making and believed in the necessity to enforce professional norms and a sense of responsibility among bureaucrats (stated in contemporary jargon, to instil pro-social values of 'public service motivation'). One finds in Olsen's 'institutionalist' approach that also challenges the rationalist principal–agent framework a similar attention 'to processes of socialization, internalization, identification, and habituation that make actors accept codes of conduct specifying appropriate behavior of different roles in different situations as legitimate' (Olsen, 2017: 50).

bureaucracy's room to manoeuvre (Moe, 1984: 768–9). Public organizations invest resources to handle accountability challenges and invent coping mechanisms that balance tensions.[24] Recent experimental research has demonstrated that accountable agents seek to prioritize among conflicting expectations, unsurprisingly, with the threat of sanction as the most important driver of prioritization (Aleksovska, Schillemans and Grimmelikhuijsen, 2022). Dilemmatic situations in the face of 'quasi-anarchically structured' (Schillemans, 2016: 1402) webs of accountability may nevertheless also lead to what Koppell (2005) aptly called a 'multiple accountabilities disorder' (MAD), which is likely to paralyze individuals, organizations or segments thereof and cause tragic operational failures (Romzek and Dubnick, 1987; Romzek and Ingraham, 2000: see also Section 5.2).

> In a study of the initial governance structure of the Internet Corporation for Assigned Names and Numbers (ICANN), Koppell (2005) suggests conflicting accountability expectations were largely responsible for organizational dysfunctions. This corporation was expected to serve the vaguely defined community of internet users while being controlled by the US government. Conflicts have regularly arisen between technically appropriate options and contractually required options. As a result, ICANN behaved inconsistently and frequently reversed course, ultimately leading to loss of support.

Whatever its side effects, control within the state apparatus seems to have been increasing in formality, complexity, intensity and specialization.[25] This does not mean that it has necessarily gained effectiveness. Moreover, the description of political-administrative relations must be put into context: multiple country-specific trajectories of administrative regimes exist and reflect historically rooted regional traditions, such as that of Anglo-American, Scandinavian or Germanic countries or states in Latin Europe that mostly followed the Napoleonic model (Peters, 2021).

4.2 Administrative Reforms and Accountability

Reform trajectories have diverged to some extent across states, as they are conditioned by their domestic institutional context, power balance and path dependencies, but also within them.[26] However, for the sake of brevity, the

---

[24] See Schillemans (2015) and Piatak et al. (2018).

[25] This was shown in detail regarding the United Kingdom by Hood et al. (1999).

[26] Pollitt and Bouckaert (2017) identified four main trajectories: maintaining, modernization, marketization and minimization.

emphasis in this section is on the common shifts in accountability patterns that have taken place in recent decades. Many reforms have indeed been driven, inter alia, by the common expectation that enhanced accountability would lead to better performance, and this in turn should provide more legitimacy to the state. These reforms originated in a critique of the bureaucracy, often portrayed as too powerful and obsessed with rules to the detriment of results and efficiency, and aimed at greater responsiveness to the needs of service users. For that purpose, one major change concerning accountability was the shift from legalism to managerialism that occurred under the banner of New Public Management (NPM) reforms.

Without being completely replaced, compliance accountability that traditionally focuses on institutional rules and formal procedures to be followed was supplemented by performance accountability.[27] Focusing thus on output quality and problem-solving capacity and supported for that purpose by evaluation instruments such as satisfaction surveys and quantitative indicators, accountability also moves 'downwards' to become 'proximate' with target populations in the role of accountability forums. The feedback of – often loosely defined – societal stakeholders, such as more or less organized 'users' or 'clients' directly affected by public services, is strongly valued. More or less institutionalized modes of 'social' or 'civil' accountability should facilitate the formulation of appropriate policy measures and enhance public trust in government (Brummel, 2021; Sørensen and Torfing, 2021). In a sense, similar results are expected from the accountability of the administration to service users at the microlevel to what we expect from electoral accountability at the macrolevel: better responsiveness to the needs of target populations, leading in turn to 'output legitimacy'.

Nevertheless, there is no compelling evidence that changes in accountability processes improve performance: indeed, 'empirical studies observe tensions, ambiguities, contradictions and unintended consequences' (Jann, 2016: 41).[28] This happens for various reasons. For example, performance expectations can be unstable and conflict with each other. Furthermore, for such accountability mechanisms to foster improvements in terms of policy, citizens must highly value performance, but they may have other priorities and ignore evaluation opportunities. It is quite plausible that people are not attentive to performance information, especially if they do not feel strongly affected by the assessed organization or service. In addition, their judgement may be subject to bias (as already noted in Section 2)

---

[27] Interestingly, experimental studies suggest that being accountable for processes is actually associated with fewer dysfunctions than being accountable for outcomes (Hall, Frink and Buckley, 2017). Outcome accountability increases individual stress, as managers have limited influence on the outcomes of their decisions, and stress reduces attentional capacity and increases judgemental inconsistencies. See Ossege (2012) for a partial confirmation of such concerns.

[28] See also Christensen and Lægreid (2015).

if they have difficulty identifying policy workers (Bertelli, 2016) or if the information provided – such as quantitative indicators – is manipulated. For instance, this may happen when the media publish league tables even if this kind of publicity was not the purpose of performance assessment (Pollitt, 2015).

More importantly, service users are asked to evaluate performance, while aspects of service provision become less transparent, making evaluation more difficult. Digitization is a case in point: the – sometimes insidious – development of 'algorithmic regulation' (Yeung and Lodge, 2019), that is, decision-making informed by artificial intelligence, exacerbates information gaps.

Busuioc (2021) reminds us that artificial intelligence algorithmic systems have become increasingly ubiquitous in the public sector of developed countries and permeate our lives in subtle yet profound ways. Algorithm results now serve as aides to human decision-making and influence high-stakes matters, including health care, education, risk assessment and law enforcement. Such results have human consequences, including harmful ones on crucial aspects of life, such as liberty, privacy or welfare. Not only do automated systems largely dictate which neighbourhoods require more policing, which households need financial or educational support, and who is likely to commit fraud or crime, but they also may reproduce existing patterns of race, gender or lifestyle discrimination and lead to unfair outcomes. For instance, an algorithm widely used by courts in the United States to predict recidivism has been found to be biased against black defendants, and facial recognition algorithms display much higher error rates for minorities, potentially leading to false arrests and discrimination against already marginalized groups when used in policing.

Although the problems described by Busuioc raise important accountability questions, it is usually difficult to identify the logic behind algorithmic decisions and to correct the biases and unintended consequences of the use of algorithms. Meaningful oversight and malfunction diagnosis are burdened due to the large deficits in expertise that affect lay audiences and, at times, even the algorithm users within the public service, whose faith in these systems may be undue. Algorithmic outputs result from the value choices of system designers, who thereby indirectly become part of the policy-making process. However, such choices and parameters are usually not explicitly spelled out and made open to assessment by outsiders (e.g., stakeholder groups negatively affected by decisions based on algorithms), so it is difficult for them to understand and contest these choices. As explained by Busuioc (2021), algorithmic accountability first implies critically scrutinizing how the algorithmic results are reached, but this process often remains opaque. What is more, one needs to understand the role algorithmic inputs play in human decisions: for example, automated tools can serve as 'moral buffers' for humans to shift the blame and evade responsibility over a decision. In other words, accountability becomes very demanding when one has to unpack both algorithmic processes and the human–algorithm interaction. It is therefore not surprising that (as suggested by survey data: König *et al.,* 2022) people are willing to trade away algorithmic transparency for small gains in effectiveness, even in sensitive areas such as policing.

Perhaps even more fundamentally, the shift to accountability downwards is not uncontroversial from a democratic point of view, although participatory forms of accountability can be seen as positive at first glance. For instance, one may find it legitimate if feedback is provided above all by those with intense preferences on policy issues and consider that stakeholder voices should count most because they express the views of those directly affected. However, this kind of social accountability may also be normatively problematic regarding the credibility of the claims of affectedness, which can be contested, and regarding inclusiveness, as unlike citizens' votes, stakeholders' voices are not equally distributed across society.[29] It becomes questionable in such a context to what extent the ballot box continues to be an accountability mechanism 'that has any direct impact on the day-to-day operations of government' (Rock, 2020: 26), while it is not certain that participatory accountability provides satisfactory opportunities for redress. In the case of infrastructure policies, for instance, stakeholder accountability gives an advantage to groups claiming to experience negative externalities that are geographically concentrated, with the risk that diffuse interests are neglected. In addition, those who complain about costs and possibly succeed in receiving compensation may come to enjoy benefits in the future that are less foreseeable in the present (Jordana, 2017). This raises important issues about social accountability being forward-looking, having procedures elaborate enough to consider the intertemporal dimension and perhaps needing to be particularly demanding for decisions that are difficult to reverse.

Such concerns can nevertheless be relativized if we keep in mind that downwards accountability to service users does not replace the hierarchical accountability of the bureaucracy upwards, grounded in the traditional delegation chain. Input from service users is primarily expected to provide more accurate information about performance to management and political superiors, who can process this kind of information to distinguish between organizations and employees that perform well and those that do not and who can use incentives (such as

---

[29] What is more, as organization in advocacy groups is often a prerequisite for feedback of service users to be effective, collective action problems may arise.

performance pay) to reward those that contribute to good performance. Hence, a crucial question is how accountability downwards has impacted control from the top, but the answer is not straightforward. On the one hand, it may be asserted that bureaucracies have gained autonomy in their day-to-day operations to better adjust to the demands of service users: it has been frequently argued that politicians should 'steer' but not 'row' and should let managers manage. On the other hand, apart from the fact that the focus on performance also empowers auditing institutions as accountability forums, politicians can use performance evaluations for their own strategic goals. Moreover, the formal separation of politics and administration makes it easier for politicians to blame managerial failure for their own errors, especially as managers lose anonymity in a context of increased media attention: the 'agency strategy' that is part of 'blame games' (Hood, 2010).

Evidence from a survey experiment involving local elected officials in Denmark showed that the provision of information on performance makes them more willing to attribute causal responsibility to administrative management, but only in cases of low performance, suggesting a negativity bias in the attribution of responsibility (Nielsen and Moynihan, 2017).

However, it has also been argued that public managers are inclined to shift the blame upwards to their political principals because their loyalty to their superiors may be less strong than concerns about their own reputations (Moynihan, 2012). In addition, managers' discretion is not necessarily impacted by the risk of a negativity bias. For example, even in situations in which the media and political agendas reinforce each other by focusing on emotionally loaded aspects of policy-making related to public safety issues, the regulatory agenda remains insensitive, focusing on factual information and following its own course (Opperhuizen, Klijn and Schouten, 2020). Moreover, managers' vulnerability is reduced by the fact that they can game the system. Although 'measurementitis' has often involved enormous costs – the growth of an industry of specialists – it frequently has not lived up to expectations, as Pollitt (2015) showed about the UK National Health Service. Bureaucrats can resort to presentational strategies and stage management, conspicuously displaying signs of conformity to the proclaimed goals that do not reflect actual performance.

These unexpected effects of disaggregation have not remained unnoticed: they made the governmental centre 'strike back'[30] and led to new post-NPM waves of reforms, mainly intended to remedy coordination deficits, such as the 'joined-up' or 'whole-of-government' initiatives. New reforms often did not

---

[30] See, for example, Dommett and Flinders (2015) on the United Kingdom.

replace previous ones but were added to them in a layering process that followed a piecemeal logic. This harmed the clarity of responsibility because the successive reforms have been associated with different, if not contradictory, goals. The correct operation of accountability mechanisms presupposes that politicians can easily decode managers' conduct, whereas confusing goal statements obviously complicate the accomplishment of this task (even though produced by politicians themselves!). It suffices to consider that it is very difficult to reconcile the objectives of empowering service users, freeing managers and optimizing political control (Lægreid, 2014).

4.3 Network Governance and Accountability

Organizational complexity did not grow only due to the layering of reforms pursuing sometimes contradictory objectives. It also grew because reform endeavours, apart from seeking to delegate operational tasks to administrative segments closer to the frontline, consisted of the horizontal disaggregation of service provision, with public–private partnerships and outsourcing, and in the delegation of regulatory missions to independent agencies.

The policy process is often interactive, polycentric and unavoidably messy, with policy complexity mirroring and responding to societal and problem complexity. Political decisions are formulated or implemented through bargaining or deliberation between actors who 'coopete' in diffuse policy networks, involving not only politicians and administrators but also interest representatives, stakeholders and experts (independent or members of advocacy coalitions). Therefore, governance becomes less public, less vertical and more interdependent (Willems and Van Dooren, 2017). 'Coproduction' or 'collaborative governance' are the usual descriptions of such policy-making modes, referring to collaboration with non-governmental actors, vertical intergovernmental cooperation across jurisdictional layers or a combination of both (Ansell and Gash, 2008; Emerson, Nabatchi and Balogh, 2012).[31] In the face of wicked problems – characterized by unclear or controversial definitions, interdependent and uncertain causal chains, multiple stakeholders with competing values and interests, and unpredictable consequences[32] – there are undeniable practical advantages of collaborative governance with regard to policy effectiveness and acceptance. Sometimes, collaborative modes have been adopted to remedy the flaws of purely managerialist governance, and in many cases, collaborative governance also has normative value

---

[31] See, in the same *Elements* series, Cairney, Heikkila and Wood (2019), who treated simple accounts of policy-making as popular but misleading fictions or myths.

[32] Fuzziness is not only a characteristic of wicked problems: it seems to also affect the definitions thereof (Peters, 2017).

with respect to pluralism and inclusiveness. However, from a democratic perspective, it is problematic if elected officials are unevenly engaged in collaborative policy-making arenas, as shown by a comparative study of a large number of cases across countries and jurisdictional levels (Sørensen et al., 2020). The most influential actors may not be officially authorized to make collectively binding decisions: they may not be visible, possibly leading to errors in the allocation of responsibilities, or may be unelected, so that the wielding of power is divorced from democratic accountability.

The movement towards collaborative governance is prominently manifested in the advent of various modes of cooperation in public service delivery. Reforms have often led to the replacement of direct administration by inter-organizational arrangements and contractual relationships with third parties: these are suppliers of services that are more or less external to the public bureaucracy, such as hybrid bodies, for-profit and non-profit organizations, to which public policy tasks are outsourced or with which they are conducted in partnership. Such configurations are challenging for the exercise of account-ability because the strict lines of command and control are blurred and some-times disrupted (Nguyen, Rawat and Morris, 2020; Triantafillou and Hansen, 2022). It becomes necessary in such a context 'to ask whether private contrac-tors should be treated as part of the government apparatus for the purposes of holding them accountable for the exercise of public power' (Rock, 2020: 19). More control may be suitable, as it is plausible that the interests of external suppliers and their staff's values differ from those of public organizations. At the same time, contract monitoring is complicated. It becomes difficult to resolve conflicts through hierarchical channels, and the foreseen sanctions are difficult to implement (Girth, 2014). What used to be internal bureaucratic disputes become externalized, possibly leading to litigation, so this is yet another driving factor of the empowerment of courts as accountability forums, as discussed in Section 3.

Research on hybrid entities endowed with public-service tasks reveals that such entities adhere to a plurality of normative frames (Denis, Ferlie and Gestel, 2015; Skelcher and Smith, 2015) so that their accountability obligations com-bine public with market, vertical with horizontal and formal with non-mandatory elements.

Jantz et al. (2018) study how contracting out and the 'marketization' of public employment service functions (to encourage labour market 'activation') affect accountability. They observe different forms of the coexistence of instruments of market accountability, such as financial incentives through contracts and price competition, with democratic and administrative forms of accountability. In Denmark, the market accountability regime has not been fully implemented, and the combination of administrative and market accountability turned out to be very difficult and involved high transaction costs. In Germany, this combination led to inconsistencies, resulting in increased governmental regulation and the addition of new accountability layers. In the United Kingdom, despite the relative ineffectiveness of market mechanisms, no public reregulation has occurred, and the monitoring of contractual compliance by outside bodies has been limited by lack of transparency. However, performance information made available for the purpose of market accountability has been used in public campaigns to name and shame service providers.

The case of market accountability, which has the particularity of being based on the 'exit' option instead of 'voice' and deliberation (Mulgan, 2000b), is instructive. On the one hand, it is not without merit: in some countries, organizations, including public entities such as hospitals and schools, *de facto* compete with each other for service provision, and consumer sovereignty imposes discipline on providers and motivates them to meet performance targets (Peters, 2014: 219). On the other hand, it has been observed that clients use the 'exit' option as a threat to force staff to break professional rules (Klenk and Cohen, 2019). Hence, staff members face dilemmas and feel that they serve many masters. In particular, for-profit service providers must 'take into account customers' demands in order to survive in an economically competitive environment' (Sager, Thomann and Hupe, 2020: 810). For example, competing certifiers face strong pressure from regulatees if they are simultaneously their source of income, and regulatees may opt for the most cost-effective among the competing certifiers, leading to a decline of regulatory standards (Thomann, Hupe and Sager, 2018).

Finally, collaborative arrangements in general, and even more so informal policy networks that lack codification and visibility, are particularly prone to the 'many hands' problem of shared responsibility (Thompson, 1980). Mutual accountability may be developed between the multiple actors that participate in governance networks, and it does have epistemic value if these actors interact densely, share information and deliberate. We may be in the presence of a 'tangled web' of accountability ties that link actors together (Romzek, LeRoux and Blackmar, 2012), some of them formal, such as contracts, and others informal, related to norms of reciprocal obligations developed in interpersonal dynamics and to the ensuing unofficial rewards and sanctions.

However, although the social pressure to comply with expectations from peers can be a powerful regulator of actors' behaviour, this form of 'community' accountability (Koliba, Mills and Zia, 2011: 214) is not tantamount and may even be detrimental to public accountability (Papadopoulos, 2007: 480–3). The exercise of control may prove challenging for outside audiences anyway if they are confronted with wicked issues characterized by complex and uncertain causalities. This exercise is made even more difficult if such issues are addressed by policy networks operating without clear rules (Cristofoli et al., 2022), regardless of the merits of fuzzy governance structures with regard to creativity and flexibility. The same happens when the most relevant negotiations take place behind closed doors, while public meetings are staged performances with a primarily symbolic function.[33] Outsiders may not be able to assess who is responsible for success or failure and how much each actor has contributed to outcomes, so that responsibility may not be allocated in a way that does justice to each participant's contribution.[34] In view of such risks, there have even been claims that – similar to the rise of independent agencies – the advent of collaborative forms of governance results from a deliberate strategy of depoliticization that is expected to facilitate evading accountability.[35]

4.4 'Agencification' and Accountability

Another major trend is the delegation of tasks to independent agencies that have been entrusted with considerable authority, most notably over economic and risk regulation but also more generally over service delivery and policy implementation. In particular, regulatory agencies – such as competition authorities or those in charge of the utilities sector – become crucial players with strong law-making roles in their area of competence (Carpenter and Krause, 2015), so that their growth has been portrayed as 'the rise of the unelected' (Vibert, 2007). The influence of NPM doctrines is visible in several agency characteristics, such as the organizational disaggregation of centralized bureaucracies into specialized units that are considered to be more efficient, more *ex ante* operational flexibility for agency managers given their familiarity with the sector of operations, and performance contracting with the ensuing emphasis on *ex post* accountability for results (Verhoest et al., 2010).

---

[33] See, for instance, the case studies on UK 'Health and Well-being Boards' by Visram et al. (2021) but also Torfing, Sørensen and Fotel (2009) for an example of best practice in terms of public communication and external involvement in the process of building a bridge between Denmark and Germany.

[34] On blame-avoidance strategies in networks, see the case of Hurricane Katrina (Moynihan, 2012). However, experimental evidence on the potential impact of governance architecture upon the attribution of blame by citizens is mixed (Marvel and Girth, 2016).

[35] For a discussion, see Fawcett et al. (2017).

With 'agencification', political and epistemic credibility are so prioritized – and politicians considered to lack both – that large agency autonomy is considered necessary, following the model of independent central banks in charge of monetary policy. Thus, agencies become 'trustees' rather than mere delegates as envisaged by the principal–agent model: they enjoy 'fiduciary' competences, and their independence appears legitimate (Majone, 2001). Much of the reputation of independent agencies as contributors to the common good is supposed to derive precisely from their professionalism. They are thereby considered more likely to safeguard the public interest than self-interested politicians: according to this narrative, collective problem solving requires 'consistency, long-sightedness and rationality' (Eriksen, 2022: 20), while politicians primarily seek re-election and are consequently tempted to prioritize short-term considerations and constituency service. Ideally, agencies should be shielded from the intrusion of politics (Miller and Whitford, 2016). However, political reality can be more gloomy: legal provisions do not suffice to guarantee the actual independence of agencies (Hanretty and Koop, 2013); the latter can be captured by special interests;[36] and the 'agencification' process may primarily serve to evade ministerial responsibility with agencies operating as magnets that attract blame in case of misfortune (Hood, 2010).[37]

In practice, agencies are highly diverse in the kinds of tasks that they carry out, their architecture and their degree of decoupling from the traditional administrative hierarchy. Similar to other managerial reforms, agencification is subject to variation across nations and sectors. In a path-dependent logic, organizational creations are often 'acclimatized' to previously existing politico-administrative arrangements so that one encounters multiple 'implementation habitats' (Verhoest et al., 2010: 4). Not only the autonomy but also the accountability of agencies and their chief executives are context dependent.[38]

In general, the doctrine welcomes a shift from direct accountability to political superiors to more plural forms of accountability, especially for agencies

---

[36] See the contributions in Carpenter and Moss (2013).

[37] Based on findings from an experimental study, James et al. (2016) concluded that the delegation of service delivery to public managers within the state apparatus helps politicians avoid blame more than contracting out that task. See, however, Moynihan (2012) above, as well as Mortensen (2016), who argues (based on case study research) that blame shift may backfire in the face of public criticism: public managers with looser relationships to political principals find it easier to pass the buck upwards in the delegation chain.

[38] Bianculli, Jordana and Fernández-i-Marín (2015) highlight the diversity of the formal accountability regimes of regulatory bodies and the complexity of informal accountability relationships in which their executive staff is embedded. Using survey data from 342 organizations in six European countries, Overman, Genugten and Thiel (2015) identified four types of accountability arrangements in semiautonomous agencies, largely aligned with the four trajectories of administrative reform mentioned above. See also Bach et al. (2017).

endowed with regulatory tasks that should not be vulnerable to hierarchical pressure likely to undermine their autonomy. However, some authors refer to an 'autonomization paradox': autonomy is frequently accompanied by more stringent controls, so that agencies perceive themselves as being more controlled than before, especially if they manage substantial financial resources or deal with salient topics such as food safety or finance regulation (Verhoest et al., 2010: 263). There are multiple ways in which political principals continue to control agencies *ex post* and influence their operation *ex ante*, for example, through political appointments, despite formal hierarchical subordination being loosened. Political authorities continue to be *primus inter pares* in their role of accountability forums, and the extent of the shift from hierarchical accountability may have been overestimated (Hill and Lynn, 2005).

Overall, the correlation between political independence and public accountability is relatively weak, as evidenced by a large-N survey including 799 regulatory agencies in 115 countries and 17 policy sectors (Jordana, Fernández-i-Marín and Bianculli, 2018). At the same time, agencies, as typical examples of output-oriented organizations, need to justify their choices and convince various audiences about the achievement of their targets. Formally, they are subject to managerial surveillance by agency boards, financial surveillance by auditing institutions and legal surveillance by courts. Accountability to multiple forums is not without its challenges: there is a risk of redundancies that involve costs (Schillemans, 2010) but also of coordination deficits leading to conflicting claims that cause dilemmas (Schillemans et al., 2021a). In the European Union, for example, national agencies become part of a multilevel administrative space through their participation in EU-wide rule-enforcing and coordination networks. This amplifies centrifugal trends within national executives (Bach, Ruffing and Yesilkagit, 2015) because national agencies operate at arm's length from governments and tend to become 'double-hatted' by developing loyalties with respect to EU institutions (Egeberg and Trondal, 2009). The 'many eyes' problem, which may undermine the effectiveness of individual agencies' accountability, combines with the 'many hands' problem. In such a shared administrative space, responsibility is diluted, and informational asymmetries that obstruct public scrutiny are particularly difficult to overcome in multilevel settings (Brandsma and Moser, 2020: 70–2).

Agencies also need to provide justifications to stakeholders (such as firms from regulated sectors or consumer associations) and to the media, especially in the case of policy failure on hot issues: in other words, to forums that have no direct sanctioning power but whose support is necessary for their legitimacy. Tucker (2018: 259) wrote that 'enjoying insulation from day-to-day political pressures does not shield independent agency leaders from debate and challenge of various kinds' and called this 'discursive' accountability. However, even though reason-giving and deliberation are beneficial to accountability, when the targeted forums are composed of actors other than the democratic principals of the delegation chain (citizens, members of parliament and executives), this cannot be considered a functional equivalent of democratic control. For example, in the case of Dutch executive agencies, accountability towards stakeholders contributes to organizational learning but does not truly enhance democratic control (Schillemans, 2011), and critical scrutiny is impeded by the propensity of citizen councils to sympathize and gradually identify with the agency (Brummel, 2021: 1063–4). Moreover, and similar to the problem addressed above about the accountability of public organizations to stakeholders in general, the participation of those affected by agencies' activity in their scrutiny runs the risk of being limited to organized minorities that enjoy concentrated benefits or suffer concentrated costs from agencies' decisions (such as the producers or consumers of particular goods and services). Furthermore, power asymmetries at this level drive agencies to adjust their accountability practices to them (Apaydin and Jordana, 2020).

Finally, the latest research revealed two interesting trends that should be treated together, as they plausibly balance each other: the accountability activity of agencies is more intense than expected, and the monitoring activity of forums is lower than expected. First, agency management may opt to engage pro-actively in accountability activities. Depending on the type of audience, this may happen because managers believe they have a moral obligation to be held accountable or because they consider this useful for learning purposes, but management can also be animated by a consequentialist logic (de Boer, 2022). Thus, agency managers cultivate a calculated use of voluntary forms of accountability for strategic purposes as part of reputation management, credit claiming and the creation of constituency support (Busuioc and Lodge, 2016, 2017; Karsten, 2015; Koop, 2014).

Koop and Lodge (2020) found that economic regulation in the United Kingdom became increasingly politicized in the aftermath of the financial crisis, being subject to more critical media attention, parliamentary scrutiny and governmental interventionism. British economic regulators in the fields of financial markets, competition, and utilities responded by extending their communication to broader audiences – using a wider range of tools and less specialist language – and by seeking to widen consumer engagement.

Actors not held to account *de jure* may have good reasons to seek to become accountable *de facto* – through ceremonials of open public communication but also through secretive exchanges with selected target audiences behind closed doors – because accountability may not just be a constraint but also a resource. Proactive accountability contributes to a good reputation, which is in turn a firewall that shields from criticism, including when reputation is undeserved.[39] Staging 'showcase accountability' (Brummel, 2021: 1065) discourages critical scrutiny: according to experimental evidence, 'promotional symbols' compensate for poor performance by shaping citizens' attitudes (Alon-Barkat and Gilad, 2017). Once an agency's reputational authority is consolidated, it can serve as a sort of tranquillizer. If agencies come to enjoy support by influential 'coalitions of esteem' (Bertelli and Busuioc, 2021), attempts at control risk high costs, as they may be considered illegitimate and intrusive, and this induces self-restraint on behalf of accountability forums. In such a view, restraint is dictated by a consequentialist logic, but it can also be dictated by a logic of appropriateness, and in particular by deference (Maggetti and Papadopoulos, 2022). Forums may find it misplaced to criticize an organization or an individual that is highly regarded by the forum itself and in all likelihood by other socially significant audiences.

Second, as mentioned, forums may not play their monitory role, which contradicts the predictions of the principal–agent model, according to which accountability gaps are caused by agency drift. The cause here is forum drift, which often relates to information gaps and paralysis due to goal conflict (Benjamin and Posner, 2018) or to intentional inactivity because of limited time and attention and of other more pressing priorities (Schillemans and Busuioc, 2015). Policy salience seems to be necessary for forums to become active (Koop, 2011) and what counts perhaps even more is the existence of exceptional focusing events that damage the reputation of agencies by subjecting them to 'emotionalized blame attribution' (Wood et al., 2022). Now, if the problem is not so much of a failing agent but of a failing principal or forum, what happens to agency accountability to the broader public as a forum? Even parent ministries may not have the expertise to fully grasp the implications of the highly diverse and often technically, legally or operationally complex decisions made by agencies, or at least this is what agency managers tend to think (Schillemans et al., 2021b). How many ordinary citizens even know about the existence of agencies as distinct organizational 'species'? Such concerns echo the findings of election studies that challenge citizens' capacity to hold

---

[39] Research also started focusing on the reputational concerns of accountability forums: see Tidå (2022) on the European Court of Auditors which, concerned with its visibility, seeks to generate audience attention.

elected officials accountable with retrospective voting (see Section 2). However, these concerns are even more serious in the case of agencies because several among them, and many bureaucratic organizations and policy networks more generally, are much less visible to the public, notwithstanding their influence on decision-making.

Overall, the developments in this section confirm that, in view of the political role of bureaucracy, addressing issues related to the accountability thereof is necessary to capture the way the governmental process works in practice. However, after decades of research on administrative reform, the image of such accountability is complex, if not at times contradictory. Reform processes have affected accountability relations in different directions, and the outcomes appear to be highly context dependent and uncertain. Ultimately, it is indeed striking how much the picture of the accountability of administrative organizations and agents contrasts with the relative simplicity of the model of electoral accountability that connects elected politicians to the citizenry. The surprising thing in view of these considerations is that – at a macro level – the 'thermostatic' mechanism continues to operate in democratic systems. It triggers governmental responsiveness to the preferences of public opinion (as we saw in Section 2), although studies of electoral accountability do not capture the intricacies of the input, output and feedback processes leading to these adjustments.

5 Managing Accountability in Monitory Democracy

Several works emphasize that policy actors are currently under constant pressure to publicly justify their conduct and to convince stakeholders of their performance. In his path-breaking study of *The Audit Society*, Power (1999) criticized the growth of an industry of checking in many areas of social life, caused by rising demands for accountability and control and often leading to unforeseen dysfunctional consequences.[40] Keane (2009: 688) offered a more positive account in his book on 'monitory' democracy, in which he pointed out 'the rapid growth of many different kinds of extra-parliamentary, power scrutinising mechanisms'. He referred, in particular, to 'guardian' type institutions that use their claimed neutrality to appear as protectors of the public interest (see also Sections 3 and 4) and to participatory mechanisms involving advocacy groups that act as 'surrogates' (Rubenstein, 2007) in their monitoring roles for the various populations and interests that they claim to represent. This section

---

[40] There are few tests of that claim. A recent one on the Canadian government concluded that the 'explosion' indeed took place, although it is less perceptible in the last years and did not expand to all public services (Liston-Heyes and Juillet, 2022).

scrutinizes political accountability in a context of mediatization that bolsters monitory democracy, before focusing on the exercise of accountability in particularly critical moments.

5.1 Public Governance in Audience Democracy: Mediatization and Its Limits

In his book, Keane praised the virtues of monitory democracy, which puts governors under stress, but one should be cautious about the genuine democratic credentials of the accountability forums that thereby increase in importance. This applies not only to frequently technocratic guardian institutions but also to cause groups that do not necessarily reflect the public's preferences. In 'advocacy' democracy (Dalton, Cain and Scarrow, 2003), 'the advantages of education, income, and other unequally distributed resources are more likely to translate into patterns of over- and underrepresentation' (Urbinati and Warren, 2008: 405). Furthermore, frequently neither is there an identifiable constituency that delegates *ex ante* its oversight role to surrogates, nor are the affected communities in a position to sanction them *ex post* if they are not satisfied with the way they fulfilled their tasks (this applies even more in the case of elusive reference groups such as 'future generations'). It may even happen that those who are supposed to be represented are uninformed about the actions that surrogates claim to undertake in their favour, or they may ignore the sheer existence of the defenders of their cause.[41]

A recent comparative study of governmental accountability portrayed the expansion and rising impact of various accountability forums in different types of regimes (Germany, Russia and Bulgaria) as an 'accountability turn' that takes place in the 'media age' (Dimova, 2020). Alongside the official watchdog institutions and other self-authorized monitory bodies, the media play a crucial role by acting as 'fire alarms'. What precisely does this metaphor mean? In their famous study of congressional oversight over the bureaucracy in the USA, McCubbins and Schwartz (1984) showed that, instead of dedicating considerable time and energy to actively controlling bureaucrats through ongoing scrutiny ('police patrolling'), members of Congress rationally opt for intermittently relying on third parties that alert them and draw their attention to problematic situations. In other words, the surveillance of the fulfilment of *de jure* delegation mandates is *de facto* delegated to trusted external actors. Although the media have no formal competence to sanction, when they 'bark', they can spark reactions from audiences – such as voters or parliamentarians – that do have the power to

---

[41] For a more optimistic account of the conditions under which nonelectoral mechanisms can secure democratic representation, see Fossheim (2022).

activate sanctioning ('biting') mechanisms, confirming that accountability forums are resource interdependent.[42] Governing actors operate under the shadow of not only vetoes and formal sanctions but also media criticism; therefore, they also try to anticipate media reactions and to preempt negative coverage by strategically adjusting their *modus operandi* and sometimes by engaging more deeply in self-reflective processes (Jacobs and Schillemans, 2016: 29).

Media's rising influence on politics has been highlighted by Bernard Manin (1997) with his emphasis on the shift of representative government from party to 'audience' democracy, in which politics is personalized and campaigning becomes permanent in a context of fluctuating and eroding partisan loyalties. Relatedly, political communication specialists refer to the mediatization of politics (Esser and Strömbäck, 2014), which means political actors are more heavily dependent on media judgement than in the past, and the media is more independent from them.

Critical media are indispensable to a well-functioning democratic polity, and mediatization can be seen as a sign of politics becoming more subject to public scrutiny. However, things are more complicated: the effective accountability exercise requires that forums be provided with accurate information, but the information provided by the media system may be skewed even if the media is non-partisan. The media have their own agendas, and the filter of newsworthiness guides the media logic. This problem is particularly acute with the tabloid press, which, apart from simplifying reality and treating political matters superficially, adopts a predominantly populist style of reporting that consists of attributing blame to elites (Hameleers, Bos and de Vreese, 2019). Commercial media overemphasize scandals that testify – according to them – to misconduct and lack of probity, frequently calling for redress that requires 'heads to roll'. At the same time, media coverage may be of short duration, as the media may be inclined to jump over to the next newsworthy event (Kuipers and 't Hart, 2014: 591). Investigative journalists search for blunders that signal lack of competence or negligence on the part of politicians or public administrators, and seldom do they demonstrate interest in policy success that tends to be seen as business as usual. This has led Flinders (2012: chapter 6), a leading specialist in the study of accountability, to deplore the advent of a blame culture and to criticize the role of inquisitive and predatory media in fuelling a climate of undeserved suspicion vis-à-vis office holders and propagating cynical views of politics. However, overgeneralizations should be avoided, as the political communication literature concludes that the presence of deleterious media

---

[42] In addition, the media amplify formal accountability processes (e.g., parliamentary hearings): by reporting on the processes, they make them accessible to the general public (Jacobs and Schillemans, 2016: 34).

effects is contingent on the media system type (e.g., more or less commercialized, etc.) that prevails in each country (Papadopoulos, 2012).

Whatever the evaluation of media power, the media can now be seen as a 'player in their own right' (Grossman, 2022: 446) because the reputation that they have to establish good and bad reputations is something politicians tend to include as a variable in their calculations and choices. This happens even though media power may be overestimated, considering that the public often does not count media among the most highly trusted actors. Politicians and parties compete to best meet what they perceive to be media expectations through presentational strategies of 'self-mediatization', which they deploy under the guidance of communication specialists. Moreover, we have seen in Section 4 that public managers can also be targeted by highly emotional blame attribution that causes 'media stress' (Schillemans, Karlsen and Kolltveit, 2019). They become public figures, sometimes reluctantly drawn into political debates by politicians eager to deflect the blame, but occasionally without the latter's blessing.

Public sector organizations, which are increasingly under the spotlight, invest substantial resources into media management and public relations tasks (Schillemans, 2012), and managers even succeed in challenging politicians' views and in developing their own persuasive narratives (Grube, 2019). However, controlling media coverage is a difficult task, and even more so with the new media's growth that makes accountability processes more personal and direct (Kuipers and Brändström, 2020: 16),[43] despite the expanding industry of communication specialists that support officials in reaching out to the public through many channels. The information on social media may be pluralist. However, it is above all extremely abundant and unmediated and becomes easily viral in the absence of the traditional media's gate-keeping role and fact-checking function, so that news management by governing actors is harder to achieve. In particular, the distortion of information is even more prominent in the arena of social media: all sorts of fake news widely circulate and receive credit in echo chambers, as people tend to interact with other people who hold similar beliefs, and confirmation bias makes them more receptive to messages that support and intensify their views. Monitoring is in a sense democratized – Vanhommerig and Karré (2014) referred to the Internet as a low-cost medium

---

[43] The authors acknowledge that more research is necessary to capture how social media influence the work of different accountability forums. It is, for example, an open question if criticism in the social media is less risky for the incumbents because of shorter duration, or more so because it is uncontrollable (Hinterleitner, 2020: 195). It can also be argued that regular use of social media is not widespread enough, although it happens that traditional media amplify criticism in the social media.

easily accessible to 'monitorial citizens and armchair auditors' – but frequently at the expense of reflexivity and genuine deliberation.

Nonetheless, monitory democracy does face structural limitations despite the rise of internet campaigns and, therefore, is not as obtrusive as suggested (for better or worse, depending on one's views). Media coverage is partial: television news, for example, operates with episodic framing; that is, it concentrates on focusing events, relates them to individuals, and narrates simple stories (Iyengar, 1991). Hence, mediatization does not penetrate the whole policy process, as shown by Adam et al. (2019).

> Adam et al. (2019) argue that political competition triggers policy development to respond to multiple social demands, leading to policy accumulation. Such accumulation induces complexity so that policy debates are confined to narrow circles, while policy issues are insufficiently addressed in the public sphere. Politicians' accountability favours policy responsiveness (as shown in the section on elections), but in the longer run, the latter can indirectly undermine public accountability, providing fertile soil for populist discourses.

Mediatization encounters limits because part of the policy-making process unfolds backstage and is not visible to the media or because policy outputs are not suitable for media 'dramaturgy'. One can think of policy measures that are technical, lack a tangible impact on people's lives or are decided in expert forums, sometimes even (much) beyond the national level. Such policy escapes media attention – perhaps with the exception of some specialized outlets – because investing resources to report on routine and low salience issues is suboptimal in commercial terms (Hajer, 2009: 176–7). In addition, most journalists lack the background to apprehend technical issues and to become familiar with cumbersome processes. Moreover, positive treatment by the media is frequently not the primary concern for bureaucrats who care about evidence-based choices and do not seek publicity, and special interests prefer to opt for 'quiet politics' instead of going public (Culpepper, 2010). Backstage policy-making does not necessarily result from an explicit intention to shield decisions from public scrutiny, even though deliberate depoliticization strategies may also be at work, and conditions of secrecy and informality may be necessary for bargaining. However, if what happens backstage matters for policy, then serious errors in the attribution of responsibilities may occur: a comparative study of public transport and economic promotion policies in eight western European metropolitan areas concluded that elected actors are more often presented as responsible for policies ('over-responsibilised') in newspaper reporting and more often blamed for policy failures than other actors ('over-blamed': Hasler, Küebler and Marcinkowksi, 2016). Such a decoupling between the political spectacle and the reality of policy development indicates a divorce between power wielding and public accountability (Papadopoulos, 2013). We have observed this with collaborative governance (Section 4), but are things maybe different in cases of conspicuous events such as crises?

5.2 Policy Failure: Crisis Management Strategies and Their Limits

As shown in the previous section, accountability dilemmas are one of multiple causes of operational failure. One of the most prominent examples thereof in the accountability literature is that of the explosion of the space shuttle Challenger in 1986, which has been explained in part by NASA's efforts to manage diverse legitimate, albeit conflicting, pressures and expectations (Romzek and Dubnick, 1987).[44] The management of natural disasters has also been associated with failures in accountability regimes, such as in the poorly coordinated and insufficient emergency responses and recovery actions in the aftermath of Hurricane Katrina in 2005.

Koliba, Mills and Zia (2011) studied the breakdown of the collaborative governance network that had been at work following Hurricane Katrina and related the lack of crisis-coping capacity to multiple accountability deficits in the network's hybrid accountability regime. They pointed out crucial gaps with regard to multiple accountabilities: democratic (elected officials and governmental agencies saw other actors as chiefly responsible), administrative (lack of clarity of responsibility, poor design of contracts and delays due to rigid procedures), professional (dearth of expertise and inadequate training), collaborative (information gaps and communication failures), and consumer accountability (to the mostly poor and powerless residents).

Dealing with the same disaster, Moynihan (2012) uncovered that crisis response network members deployed blame avoidance strategies.[45] Following this line of research, this section addresses accountability after perceived failure, regardless of whether this means failure to prevent a crisis or to manage its consequences properly. Does accountability work when it is, arguably, mostly needed? The answer is not straightforward: accountability processes can both unsettle and transform orders as well as maintain them (Olsen, 2017).

---

[44] See Romzek and Ingraham (2000) for a similar analysis of the crash in Croatia in 1996 of the military transport plane carrying the United States Secretary of Commerce.

[45] For a more nuanced account, see Boin, Brown and Richardson (2019).

Crisis situations can be defined as 'highly negative and disruptive events or episodes characterized by threat, urgency, and uncertainty' (Kuipers and Brändström, 2020: 3). Whatever the origin of events defined as critical (natural disaster, external attack or operational deficiencies),[46] these events undermine public trust in the capability or probity of office-holders if public opinion comes to believe that they are responsible for the mishap or have not dealt adequately with its consequences (Kuipers and 't Hart, 2014: 589). Elected executive members, and increasingly unelected top public managers, are in the spotlight and become an easy target whenever public opinion is dominated by the perception that something went wrong. Obviously, crises can be exploited politically: 'crises need a face, and political executives provide those' (Kuipers and Brändström, 2020: 10).[47]

Demands for explanations may be addressed by formal bodies, such as inspectorates or ad hoc investigation commissions, which rely on professional standards to identify – normally in a dispassionate manner – the possibly highly complex causal processes that led to failure and to draw lessons for the future. Office-holders can expect scrutiny from these bodies to allow them 'to get out of the limelight'(Kuipers and t'Hart, 2014: 596) and, ultimately, to appease protest. However, the independence and discretion that these bodies enjoy in their operations may be disturbing for office-holders, so that the relations with them 'are full of ambiguity and latent tensions' (Kuipers and t'Hart, 2014: 592) and oscillate between cooperation and stonewalling. In addition, even if office holders have the tools to shape and exert control over formal accountability procedures, criticism by investigative bodies is considered more credible than positive appraisal, so that stigma cannot be easily avoided (Kuipers and 't Hart, 2014: 597). Moreover, in audience democracy, the media act as catalysts (Boin, McConnell and 't Hart, 2008: 21), frequently attracted by the newsworthiness of policy failure and – especially the tabloid press and commercial TV channels – animated by a negativity bias in their tone. Postcrisis accountability processes are usually particularly harsh, as account-holders such as opposition parties or victim organizations formulate highly demanding claims that require sustained efforts in terms of justification and manifest an appetite for drastic sanctions.[48] As disasters are judged intolerable, crises are test cases for the accountability of policy-makers (Boin et al., 2005: 124).

---

[46] See Boin, McConnell and 't Hart (2008) for different types of crises.

[47] As shown in Section 2, less sophisticated voters were more likely to disproportionately focus the blame for the inadequate response to Hurricane Katrina on President G. W. Bush.

[48] See the example of parliamentary accountability mechanisms in the United Kingdom leading to crisis escalation, with opposition parliamentarians 'playing to the gallery' in conjunction with sensationalist media reporting (Stark, 2011: 1157–61).

On the one hand, public authorities are exposed to stress caused by an upsurge of accountability demands and sometimes to a spiral of escalating criticism so that they are in a great need to calm protests.[49] On the other hand, they are not powerless: postfailure strategic behaviour 'is a pivotal task of crisis leadership' (Boin et al., 2005: 103) and consists of coping creatively with pressing claims for transparency, explanations and possibly sanctions. Crises are extraordinary, often complex and dynamic phenomena, so that ambiguity and uncertainty leave space for conflicts of interpretation: facts are disputed, the causalities of events are difficult to disentangle, the division of tasks between 'principals' and 'agents' is challenged and the pertinence of evaluative standards – perhaps even that of the existing accountability routines – is contested (Olsen, 2017). Therefore, one needs to win the battle of meaning-making by imposing one's definition of the situation in the contests between frames and counterframes regarding the accidental or structural origin of crises, as well as their severity and their implications (Boin, 't Hart and McConnell, 2008). For instance, it may be unclear or controversial if and to what extent public authorities must be blamed for the casualties, and proof of that responsibility may require time-consuming investigative procedures and even court rulings. As even the functioning of independent public inquiries and their conclusions may be shaped by postcrisis politics, there is ample room (and need) for increasingly professional impression management. Presentational strategies extend from dramatization, escalation and overresponsibilization – by the opposition, critical media and cause groups – to problem denial and minimization with the use of 'defensive scripts' (Kuipers and 't Hart, 2014: 593) by those accused of responsibility for failure. Does blame avoidance then help win the accountability battle?[50]

Christopher Hood (2015) first made the explicit connection between the literature on public accountability and the literature on blame avoidance. The latter posits that it is crucial for politicians and public managers to manoeuvre to shield themselves and reduce reputational damage. If blame cannot be proactively avoided,[51] it may be worth seeking occasions to pass the buck, sacrifice scapegoats, or diffuse the blame and 'circle the wagons' (Weaver, 1986: 388–9).

---

[49] This may be called the cathartic function of accountability that operates as a purification ritual: see Kuipers and Brändström (2020).

[50] Presentational strategies may also include credit taking, with attempts to associate positive events with governmental action through sound, perhaps also heroic, crisis management. Nevertheless, Weaver (1986), in his foundational piece on blame avoidance, considered that politicians are more blame minimizers than credit maximizers because of their own loss aversion and voters' negativity bias.

[51] In particular, the literature on welfare state retrenchment focuses on policy-makers' strategies that aim to preempt the risk of electoral blame, such as the concealment or dissemination of losses: see Vis (2016) for a literature review. Hinterleitner (2017) pleads for more integration

The literature provides nuanced conclusions on the capacity to evade accountability by deflecting blame. For example, the intense and negative media scrutiny that characterizes postcrisis situations correlates with cases of resignation, but politicians with more experience, higher precrisis credibility and a thorough understanding of the rules of the game tend to be better shielded (see Kuipers and Brändström, 2020: 13–15).

Unclear causal relations and ambiguous allocation of tasks are theoretically prone to blame-shift strategies, but comparative research tends to show that the outcome of such strategies is uncertain and context dependent. Hood, Jennings and Copeland (2016) compared how heads of government in the USA, the UK, Ireland and Canada behaved when they faced media blame for their personal conduct. Although the authors found evidence that office-holders admit responsibility only after problem or responsibility denial are exhausted as presentational strategies ('staged retreat'), they doubt the effectiveness of blame management in dampening the firestorm. In his study of policy controversies that gave birth to blame games in the UK, Germany and Switzerland, Hinterleitner (2020) distinguished between 'high stakes' and 'below the radar' blame games leading to different outcomes. He found that the public salience of issues and the institutional terrain, including informal and implicit game rules, shape the space in which conflict management occurs by providing blaming gateways and barriers against blame. In the British political system, for example, restrictive conventions about resignation (and more generally responsibility attribution) 'clearly benefit incumbents during blame games' with limited incentives for the government to amend failed policies; in contrast, in Germany, extensive conventions of resignation are, among others, 'conducive to creating a rather aggressive blame game that centers on political incumbents' (Hinterleitner, 2020: 186). This stands at odds with the conventional knowledge about the conflictual Westminster-style bipartisan politics in the United Kingdom and the more accommodative style of German politics related to coalition government and institutional fragmentation.

Needless to say, the existence of a delegation chain can help deflect blame towards 'lightning rods' and thus offers policy-makers a 'protective coating' (Boin et al., 2005: 118), as in the United Kingdom, where 'media attention and opponent attacks overwhelmingly focus on administrative actors and entities' due to relatively low direct governmental involvement (Hinterleitner, 2020: 186). Blame-shifting frames are also more credible in situations in which multiple jurisdictional levels (Maestas et al., 2008) or networks of actors

---

between research on blame caused by unpopular policies and research on blame caused by policy failure.

(Moynihan, 2012) are involved, often characterized by lack of responsibility clarity. However, a blame shift may not suffice, and in the end, it may be necessary to admit responsibility for the mishaps and to culminate in a restorative rhetoric (Boin et al., 2005: 123). Interestingly, the most effective strategy, according to a meta-study, is self-disclosure of failures, apologies and corrective action, but taking such steps is much more painful than denying the problem. Hence, denial of responsibility is the framing that is most commonly used in response to threats and criticism, even though it is the least effective one (see Kuipers and Brändström, 2020: 12)

The analysis should also include the long-term consequences of postcrisis accountability, but it is difficult to anticipate if a crisis will be 'fast-burning' with a return to 'business as usual' or if there will be 'a crisis after the crisis'. This depends, for instance, upon how quickly public attention will move on to other concerns, and timing matters more generally if we think, for example, of the tighter or looser connection with the electoral cycle (Boin, McConnell and 't Hart, 2008). According to some literature, the 'long-shadow' crisis, in which 'turning the page' is impossible, is the norm and elite 'reinvigoration' the exception (Boin et al., 2005: 104–5; Boin, 't Hart and McConnell, 2008: 289, 294).[52] Crises seem to be critical junctures that provide opportunity windows and fertile ground for the claims of opposition actors and reformist advocacy groups: indeed, 'crises can make, break, or transform political and public service careers, agency mandates and reputations, and policy paradigms' (Kuipers and 't Hart, 2014: 590).

However, even authors who highlight the enduring effects of crises are nuanced. Although cases of overreaction exist (Maor, 2012), postcrisis action can be restricted to symbolic manipulation and paper exercises, and crises do not necessarily lead to substantial policy adjustments because a return to normalcy may be strongly desired. The need to restore the broken trust in governance capacity does not always translate into genuine learning and into the policy shifts that would be required to avoid repeated misfortune, precisely because of the political nature of the postcrisis phase (Boin, 't Hart and McConnell, 2008).[53] Postcrisis change is often incremental rather than radical (Boin, 't Hart and McConnell, 2009): for example, studying various disasters in the United States (e.g., homeland security in the case of September 11, natural

---

[52] The business administration literature is more optimistic than the political science and public administration research on the capacity to restore one's image following a failure. More cross-fertilization between these distinct bodies of work is needed (see Kuipers and Brändström, 2020).

[53] See, however, Stark (2018) for a more positive account on the learning impact of public inquiries, based on an international comparison.

catastrophes such as Hurricane Katrina, etc.), Birkland (2006) found that, for critical events to be conducive to genuine policy change, several conditions are necessary, such as event-induced media attention, issue salience for a large portion of the public, the existence of advocacy groups and the preexistence of policy ideas that can provide inspiration for reform.

Therefore, it is reasonable to subscribe to the prudent observation that accountability after crises is a process that 'leaves us with inconclusive answers to pivotal questions concerning "what works when, and for whom"' (Kuipers and 't Hart, 2014: 600). Explanations must take different interacting factors into account, namely, the nature of the crisis, the institutional and political contexts and, of course, actors' strategies. In addition, one should distinguish among the different outcomes of accountability processes. Competing agendas may coexist, causing goal conflict: for example, this can occur when a forward-looking investigatory body concerned with truth-finding seeks to analyse the causes of accidents to improve future operations, while backward-looking commercial media primarily look for culprits who will make headlines. Sanctioning office-holders is different from triggering policy change, and both may be unrelated; policy change will not have the same scope if it stems from genuine learning from failures or from superficial strategic adjustment.

In this section, emphasis was initially placed on the fact that governmental activity is put under the 'public microscope' (Kuipers and 't Hart, 2014: 592) in the context of audience or monitory democracy. Some see this as a virtuous process, but others deplore the perverse effects resulting from the negativity bias that prevails among some accountability forums, such as commercial media or opposition parties. However, many miss that low salience backstage policy-making activities are shielded from public scrutiny, so the trend towards 'hyper-scrutiny' encounters limits. In addition, even following crises or failures, policy-makers seek to control accountability processes and to deflect the blame. The success of such strategies is not ensured, which is not bad news for the role of public accountability. At the same time, some policy-makers may be under- or over-responsibilized so that the divorce between power and accountability continues to exist. As it is not certain that accountability processes trigger policy improvements, the overall contribution of public accountability to good governance in the context of audience and monitory democracy is ambivalent.

6 Perceptions Matter: Overloads and Felt Accountability

Accountability is generally praised as a virtue, and democratic theorists usually criticize its deficits. However, we also found dissenting voices, such as Power's critical take on the audit explosion accompanied by verification rituals or

Flinders' fear that the over-exposure of politicians to accountability, coupled with a negative bias in media reporting, fuels a culture of distrust that unduly undermines the legitimacy of the political system. As stated by Hall, Frink and Buckley (2017: 212), 'the effects of accountability may be nonlinear in that some accountability may be necessary to motivate but too much may cause strain reaction'. Hence, claims about the adverse consequences of accountability merit consideration, and as accountability 'pathologies' include deficits and overloads, one should ideally strive to optimize accountability. With such a goal in mind, Rock (2020) sought to identify benchmarks to assess how much accountability is necessary and sufficient and what kind of accountability arrangements are most suitable depending on their assigned purposes. Rock also developed yardsticks to rigorously evaluate the extent to which existing arrangements approximate normative expectations but acknowledged that defining an ideal accountability balance is no small task.

This section tackles the problem of accountability overloads and their consequences: accountability in excess, or too much emphasis on accountability, may become counterproductive. Public administration research primarily focuses on accountability at the organizational level. It highlights the risk of goal conflict: too narrow an emphasis on accountability to the detriment of other organizational goals can negatively affect the quality or efficiency of public services. Overreporting, for example, may induce goal displacement: it can prevent the achievement of less-well observable long-term goals, generate opportunity costs as resources are diverted from other necessary activities that are neglected, and increase transaction costs through bureaucratization (Schillemans and Bovens, 2015: 6–7). In other words, accountability comes at a price, literally and figuratively.

The organizational level is not the only one pertinent to the study of accountability, and we have seen that individuals, such as elected officials, public managers, frontline professionals or participants in collaborative networks, are also formally or informally accountable. In reality, the relationships between organizational and individual accountability are complex: one can distinguish between 'corporate' accountability in which an organization as a whole is called to account, 'hierarchical' accountability in which only the leadership of the organization is required to give account, 'individual' accountability in which individuals must give accounts for acts of the organizations to which they belong because they are considered responsible for those acts, and 'collective' accountability in which every member of an organization is (potentially) accountable (Bovens, Goodin and Schillemans, 2014: 10). Whatever the type of accountability mechanisms, it can only be effective if individuals within organizations perceive that it exists and react to its existence by adjusting their behaviour (Overman and Schillemans, 2022). Hence, it is also important to analyse the mechanisms of accountability at the individual level.

Accountability is also considered to cause a number of pathologies in individual behaviour, such as discouraging flexibility and undermining motivation (Halachmi, 2014). Facing accountability pressure, actors adopt defensive behaviour to shield themselves, which minimizes the risk of blame but impedes out-of-the-box thinking: as observed, 'accountability systems are frequently not perceived by managers as something to help the execution of public duties and organizational performance but something that discourages them from taking risks and seeking improvements' (Yang, 2012: 277, n. 4). Formalism and stereotyping are likely to prevail when blindly following the letter of the law or simulating conformity to the prescribed line of conduct (Philp, 2009: 43), for example, when members of the bureaucracy or implementing bodies game the system by manipulating performance indicators (see Section 4).

Institutional factors account for some of these pathologies; for example, the doctrine of ministerial responsibility in the United Kingdom 'has the potential to encourage a conservative, defensive style of decision-making because it encourages crisis managers to reflect upon personal risk and elite damage during policy deliberations' (Stark, 2011: 1162). However, one also needs to delve deeper into individual actors' 'mental imprint' (Overman and Schillemans, 2022: 12) simply because not all people react the same way to similar accountability pressure (Han and Robertson, 2021). It is therefore necessary to draw inspiration from studies in social and organizational psychology, which offer a fine-grained picture of the microfoundations of accountable actors' conduct. In particular, Tetlock (1991) used the politician's metaphor to explain human behaviour more generally (different from the model of the utility maximizer *homo economicus*). From this perspective, people are considered to think and act as 'intuitive politicians who seek the approval of the constituencies to whom they feel accountable' (Tetlock and Lerner, 1999: 573). Accountability thus appears to be 'the fundamental social contingency driving individual behavior and decisions ... because individuals are concerned about their image and seek approval in the eyes of others' (Hall, Frink and Buckley, 2017: 206). This happens primarily if those held accountable score high on social anxiety and perceive their audience as powerful and with strong preferences.

It is slightly ironic that the school of thought based on Tetlock's assumptions assumes that the politician's metaphor applies to life in general, yet we still do not know much about how politicians feel about their accountability obligations. Surprisingly, more is known about the properties of those who hold others accountable in democratic politics – for example, about citizens' sophistication and reflexivity (see Section 2) – than about the psychology of those who are held accountable. We do know more about the experiences of members of the bureaucracy, but it is only recently that public administration scholarship made the behavioural turn to individuals' 'felt' accountability. Felt accountability has been defined as 'the implicit or explicit expectation that one's decisions or actions will be subject to evaluation by some salient audience(s) with the belief that there exists the potential for one to receive either rewards or sanctions based on this expected evaluation' (Hochwarter et al., 2007: 227). Psychologists conduct laboratory experiments and field studies to scrutinize at the micro level how perceived accountability pressures affect individuals' cognitive and emotional states.[54] Regarding the deleterious effects of intrusive scrutiny on account-givers, social psychological research confirms that tension and exhaustion escalate when supervision is considered abusive (Breaux et al., 2008). Furthermore, this research confirms that 'decision-makers can become mired in self-justification, so anxious to defend past commitments that the majority of their mental effort is devoted to generating reasons why they are right and their would-be critics wrong' (Tetlock and Lerner, 1999: 572). For defensive bolstering to prevail, however, the accountor's past actions must be irreversible, and the accountee must be perceived as relatively hostile and intimidating, but not too much; otherwise, the accountor is more likely to capitulate.

Accountability is also likely to trigger effects that are more positive.[55] When neither the accountee nor the accountor is encumbered by strong commitments or views, accountors tend to become more self-reflective and self-critical and to develop effort-demanding patterns of thinking to anticipate and accommodate plausible objections of potential critics.[56] Furthermore, the accountors' perception of their audiences' properties influences their disposition to comply: compliance can be judged as more or less morally prescribed or considered inevitable given the costs of non-compliance. The audience's legitimacy, as evaluated by the account-giver, determines its moral authority to impose

---

[54] The strength of experimental studies is that they subject causal claims to rigorous testing. Their weakness is their limited external validity. As most of them are conducted in university classrooms, their generalizability to the messy real-world of policy-making is uncertain: see Schillemans (2016: 1413) and Aleksovska, Schillemans and Grimmelikhuijsen (2019: 6). Although students may behave as intuitive politicians, this does not make them real-world political actors or public service employees.

[55] Accountability does less so when it is moderated for different reasons, such as in the case of subjects scoring high on dogmatism measures. Although dogmatism highlights the weight of personality traits, task characteristics, professional roles and organizational conditions also moderate accountability effects; for example, Overman and Schillemans (2022: 15) expect four archetypes of civil servants to experience 'felt' accountability differently.

[56] Evidence from a systematic review of research on the behavioural effects of accountability confirms that the latter tends to lead to effortful and better-informed decision-making (Aleksovska, Schillemans and Grimmelikhuijsen, 2019: 8).

control, reducing the risk of accountability obligations being seen as excessive or unfair and, thereby, the risk of dysfunctional organizational conduct as a response. In addition, how the accountor regards the audience's expertise shapes his or her perception of the latter's ability to exercise control effectively and thus tempers the accountor's inclination to evade accountability (Overman, Schillemans and Grimmelikhuijsen, 2021).[57]

Gersen and Stephenson (2014) approached accountability dysfunctions from a different angle. Using the standard principal–agent framework to study delegation relations between citizens, politicians and bureaucrats, they singled out five types of bad policy carried out by agents (such as politicians or bureaucrats) precisely – this is important – because they are held accountable by their principals (e.g., voters or the legislature). According to the authors, the problem is that even relatively well-informed (expert) agents might be induced by conformism to select courses of action they personally do not think appro-priate. As agents care about their reputation – most notably with the purpose of staying in office or advancing their careers – they adopt coping strategies to please their principals, whose preferences they know or anticipate. Thus, they comply with the expectations of principals who are poorly informed about the consequences of the chosen policies and, therefore, are not good judges.

The authors describe such situations as 'over-accountability', which is rela-tively misleading because the dysfunctions are not due to accountability in excess but to accountability tout *court* or, more precisely, to the sheer associ-ation of accountability mechanisms with delegation.[58] As the authors point out, 'Not only do accountability mechanisms fail to remedy the agency problem inherent in representative government, they actually make the problem worse' (Gersen and Stephenson, 2014: 187). Should these mechanisms be blamed, however? If they produce wrong signals and provide inappropriate incentives, this is not because they are essentially flawed. Instead, it is because the accountability forums are prone to misperceptions and thus likely to reward wrong actions by those to whom power was delegated. Hence, the problem lies not in (over)accountability but in the poor quality of information available to the accountability forum, which does not allow for sound judgements.

Be that as it may, the authors identified the following dysfunctions: pandering (i.e., selecting a popular policy even if the agent does not believe it is in the

---

[57] For an empirical application, see Schillemans et al. (2021b). The authors investigated how control by the parent department was evaluated on an individual level by executive staff in agencies in seven European countries and the extent to which this related to perceptions of the parent department possessing sufficient expertise and being legitimate as an accountability forum.

[58] These mechanisms can be weakened with longer terms of office or permanent contracts, as the authors suggest.

principal's interest),[59] posturing (i.e., taking attention-grabbing but risky action, even if the agent finds it inappropriate), persistence (i.e., sticking to a policy, even if the agent no longer believes in it), populism (i.e., ignoring the fate of unpopular minorities or causing them harm) and, symmetrically, political correctness (i.e., adopting policies that benefit a popular cause more than the agent thinks necessary). All these dysfunctions are theoretically plausible, but are they inevitable?

Persistence, for example, is also highlighted by path-dependence theory, which attributes the difficulty of path-shifting policy change not only to the fact that major reforms can be blocked by vested interests occupying institutional veto points (Immergut, 1992) but also to office-holders' self-restraint out of the fear of electoral punishment by loss-averse constituencies of policy beneficiaries (Pierson, 1994). It is true that 'zombie ideas' may continue to prosper despite conspicuous policy failure (Peters and Nagel, 2020). However, if we consider the risky behaviour of posturing, we have seen that the public administration literature associates accountability pressure with risk-adverse behaviour. Even though psychologists do not consider the latter pervasive (Aleksovska, Schillemans and Grimmelikhuijsen, 2019: 8), their studies do not confirm the prevalence of unreflective posturing either, not to mention that the distinction between public posturing and private thought is not easy to establish (Tetlock and Manstead, 1985).

Overall, are accountable agents risk maximizers or minimizers? It may be argued that the course of action the agent choses (risk-adverse or not) ultimately depends on his or her perception of the significant others' preferences. For instance, one can understand that bureaucrats opt for closely adhering to the rules to avoid displeasing their hierarchical superiors; however, it is less clear why agents would have to adopt heroic behaviour to satisfy their principals. Of course, some voters may expect grandiose achievements from politicians, but voters can also be reassured with symbolic politics, which signal that policy-makers are determined to act without them making efforts to implement any concrete measures. We know that informational asymmetries leave room for manoeuvre so that agents can simulate compliance with principals' expectations, and principal–agent scholarship does not ignore the option of superficial 'box-ticking' and 'ceremonial' buffering (Hawkins and Jacoby, 2006: 210). This is confirmed by evidence from psychological research, according to which 'decision-makers may devote cognitive effort to thinking of ways to beat the system, to exploiting loopholes in the accountability ground rules' (Tetlock and Lerner, 1999: 572).

---

[59] See also Section 2 on the risk of electoralism.

However, there is a more fundamental criticism that affects all potential sources of bad policy because it challenges the assumption that accountable agents primarily seek to conform to what they perceive as their audiences' preferences (acceptability heuristic). This criticism is again grounded in the influential social contingency model developed in psychological research (Tetlock, 1992), which posits the ubiquity of accountability relations within which individuals work and live. The model assumes that 'accountability alters fundamental cognitive processes such as how people perceive, encode, and retrieve information' (Lerner and Tetlock, 1999: 266).[60] That is, they seek to adjust their images to what they think fits their audiences' expectations. However, the model also reveals the diversity of accountability effects on individuals, which depend 'on a complex host of moderators' (Lerner and Tetlock, 1999: 259).[61] Hence, attempts at impression management coexist with defensive bolstering, and whenever the incriminated actors are under emotional pressure and express resentment because they feel that the audience's judgement and sanctions are unjust or excessive, backfiring is possible (Lerner and Tetlock, 1999: 258–9). In that respect, Braithwaite (1997) argued that hard sanctions are self-defeating because they trigger defiance, and he consequently privileged dialogue to stimulate compliance and prevent abuses of power. Although limitations of 'big sticks' that rebound must be acknowledged, whether and under what conditions – most notably when account-givers are open to discussion and simultaneously care about their 'public-regarding self' – dialogue and persuasion are more effective remains to be proven by empirical evidence. It has been demonstrated, for instance, in a conjoint experiment conducted with British and Dutch managers that the threat of sanctions – accountability's 'hard side' – is the most powerful tool that account-holders can employ to ensure that civil servants prioritize their demands (Aleksovska, Schillemans and Grimmelikhuijsen, 2022).

Furthermore, overloads are not just a matter of quantity but also depend on the interrelationships between accountability mechanisms (Rock, 2020: 214). For example, the duplication of accountability mechanisms has merits and drawbacks. We know that if a mechanism fails, for example, if the accountor and the accountee develop incestuous relations that prevent critical scrutiny, another mechanism can take over. Braithwaite (1997) saw merits in the separation of powers through the failsafe role of multidimensional accountability mechanisms

---

[60] That text is the first systematic literature review on felt accountability; Hall, Frink and Buckley (2017) followed up and systematically surveyed the literature post-1998; Aleksovska, Schillemans and Grimmelikhuijsen (2019) covered all experimental studies investigating accountability mechanisms in the behavioural sciences.

[61] '[M]uch depends on whether the views of the prospective audience are known or unknown, on whether people learn of being accountable before or after exposure to the evidence on which they are asked to base their judgments, on whether people learn of being accountable before or after making a difficult-to-reverse public commitment' (Tetlock and Lerner, 1999: 572–3).

that follow different logics and operate in parallel. Furthermore, hearing a plurality of voices enhances the acceptance and epistemic quality of policy with the incorporation of a variety of perspectives. However, we have also seen that people may experience disarray when expectations from multiple forums conflict, and this may lead to mismanagement, accidents and crises. Even if the outcome is not disastrous, being subject to redundant controls may generate a feeling of purposelessness, and psychological research demonstrates that competing views between audiences about what should be done induce decision-evasion tactics, such as procrastination and avoiding taking any stand (Tetlock and Lerner, 1999: 575–7). Conflicts may be overcome by overrelying on a particular accountability type, but this can lead to malfunctioning, for example, if high pressure for political and hierarchical accountability weakens accountability for compliance with professional quality standards (Yang, 2012: 260). Finally, it may be easier to game the system in the face of multiple accountability forums by forging alliances with the more sympathetic or less biting forums or strategically playing forums one against the other, resulting in a loss rather than an increase of control.

Despite these problems, as already mentioned, experimental research tends to show that accountability mostly has positive effects on the quality of decision-making. It may be objected that this is less true if accountability is perceived to be in excess, but it is very difficult to agree on what 'excess' means and what conditions shape perceptions of overload and lead to pathologies.[62] Although different kinds of dysfunctional responses to pressure appear in the literature, the evidence remains inconclusive on the likelihood that pathologies of accountability occur and when. Moreover, cognitive and behavioural patterns that are discernible at the individual level cannot be easily transferred to the organizational level. There is yet another limitation: although experimental research has managed to find its way into the study of public administration, enhancing the accuracy of the evaluation of bureaucrats' conduct in the face of audience expectations, this is not yet the case for the study of other key policy-makers facing similar expectations and, above all, politicians.

7 Conclusion: Core Messages

This concluding section is divided into two sections that provide a synthesis of the essential points developed in the foregoing text and present the main takeaways.

---

[62] For example, Aleksovska, Schillemans and Grimmelikhuijsen (2019: 9) wrote in their systematic review: 'Under which conditions accountability stimulates responsible decision-making and under which it results in a decision-making deadlock and decision avoidance is not yet clear'.

7.1 Lessons Learnt on Power and Accountability

Following the introductory section, the point of departure for Section 2 on elections was the crucial role thereof as the core mechanism of democratic accountability in representative government and, therefore, as a major legitimizing device of democratic systems. Although such a function rests on solid theoretical grounds, is it also corroborated by empirical tests? Overall, competitive elections do not perform badly as the foremost channel of democratic accountability; however, the evidence is mixed. There is no agreement on whether we can consider voters as sufficiently well-equipped (or willing) to evaluate governments' past performance and subsequently reward or sanction them. For example, voters use heuristics to help them in their evaluative tasks, but it is uncertain if such shortcuts may be misleading. The evidence is also inconclusive regarding the institutional setup's impact on voters' capacity, including factors such as electoral and party systems, the composition of the executive, a divided government or the vertical separation of tasks across jurisdictions. It seems that electoral accountability works best when power is concentrated because this is associated with more clarity of responsibility. On the one hand, it may be embarrassing if it is difficult to reconcile democratic accountability with a pluralist power structure. On the other hand, it is reassuring if electoral accountability is an effective counterweight when power is concentrated (Olsen, 2017: 24).

We can also be reassured by the fact that the 'thermostatic' model seems to work in democracies. This happens most likely because governments fear (whether correctly or erroneously) the electoral sanction, are therefore incentivized to be responsive to citizens' preferences and produce policies flexible enough to adjust for opinion shifts. However, the study of electoral accountability remains relatively superficial because it is limited to the official office-holders' accountability, regardless of their actual degree of responsibility for policy outcomes, and overlooks the role of other key players, which requires a shift in focus from elections to opening up the black box of policy-making processes.

Doctrines of power separation impose institutional checks on the exercise thereof, which should bring about (self)restraint and thus prevent abuses by office-holders. Hence, Section 3 studies interinstitutional accountability: the vertical accountability of the executive and its members to parliament and the horizontal accountability between institutions that are not in a delegation relationship and are relatively equal in terms of power. Although there is no agreement on whether current trends in governance point towards a concentration of power in the hands of the executive or towards its fragmentation in polycentric networks of actors, it can be expected that both trends negatively impact – albeit for different reasons – the capacity of parliaments to control the executive. 'Deparliamentarization' refers to the declining role of parliaments, including their executive oversight function: much like individual citizens, parliamentary institutions may not be able, or even willing, to perform their role as accountability forums, so accountability deficits may not be due to agents evading blame but rather to forum passivity. Some parliaments have reacted to their loss of power, but the countertrend is not uniform. Even when parliaments 'fight back', they tend to hold the government accountable informally, with procedures of confidential accountability leading to interinstitutional bargaining that lacks transparency and undermines accountability to the public.

Equally worth mentioning is the growing relevance of rulers' horizontal accountability to unelected forums, whose coupling with electoral accountability is not without frictions. Horizontal accountability may tame electoral accountability by design, as unelected forums derive their legitimacy from their independence from political interests. Moreover, they can convert their control power into influence on policy: when an institution is horizontally accountable to another institution whose consent is needed, it is incentivized to absorb the preferences of the latter, just as office-holders are incentivized to be responsive to citizens in vertical accountability. This happens most notably with the preferences of courts, whose role as accountability forums has substantially increased with the phenomenon of 'judicialization'. The empowerment of judges is a core dimension of the 'rise of the unelected', and adjudication draws its legitimacy from the judicial process having a reputation of being depoliticized, impartial and fair. The 'law of anticipated reactions' is also at work when executives and legislatures become accountable to the courts: they seek to reach decisions that are robust to court rulings without being too remote from their own initial preferences. Although judicialization is driven by concerns about unrestricted majority power and the need to protect fundamental rights, it remains controversial. Judges cannot claim to be representative, and they are unaccountable by design to safeguard their independence. For some, this is a major challenge to the legitimacy of courts as accountability forums that gain influence in the policy proces. However, elected politicians are not powerless in the face of judicial activism; therefore, judges may also find it rational to internalize their preferences, and 'government by judges' is not unrestricted either.

Section 4 zooms into another category of key policy actors: the members of the bureaucracy. Political control over the bureaucracy seems to have become more sophisticated; however, it is not without limits, costs and collateral effects. Although upwards hierarchical accountability persists, it is difficult to say if control from the top is more effective now. Successive waves of reforms have sought to make it smarter, but they differ in their content depending on national trajectories and administrative styles. In addition, there is no clear indication that the stronger emphasis on accountability to target populations has produced the expected gains in performance and, indirectly, 'output legitimacy'. This is hardly surprising considering that administrative reforms have often been animated by conflicting goals, rendering trade-offs unavoidable: ultimately, the empowerment of service users or 'clients' has been relative, and it becomes more difficult with the recent development of algorithmic decision-making that is a black box for outsiders. Their empowerment also remains controversial from a normative point of view, so it cannot be asserted that more participatory forms of accountability lead to genuine gains in terms of democratic policy-making.

In addition, collaborative forms of governance and the outsourcing or 'copro-duction' of public services have grown in advanced democracies. On the one hand, such policy-making styles present epistemic advantages, especially in the face of wicked problems; they may enhance policy acceptance and can be valued normatively for being pluralist and inclusive. On the other hand, the issue of appropriate checks to political power wielded through hybrid governance modes and non-public actors is a real one. From a democratic point of view, it is problematic when elected politicians are not strongly engaged in collaborative policy-making arenas and unelected actors are counted among the most powerful. The exercise of power is then divorced from democratic accountability, and when the key players are unseen, the correct allocation of responsibilities is hampered. When policy-making is conducted through amorphous or informal channels, this leads to the 'many hands' problem, impeding public scrutiny. Moreover, even control by professional politicians becomes difficult when command lines are blurred and operators are dissociated from the hierarchical circuit. Furthermore, some participants in networks face multiple expectations from accountability forums with conflicting preferences, and the simultaneous presence of 'many eyes' requires developing coping strategies to deal with dilemmas: '360-degree feedback' (Behn, 2001) may lead to fuzziness and unpredictability. This kind of cross-pressure may thus cause damage to the public interest and be detrimental to democratic accountability.

A different facet of shifts in governance – and another dimension of the 'rise of the unelected' – is the diffusion of the agency phenomenon. The legitimacy of agencies is grounded not just on their expertise but also, similar to courts, on their impartiality, and their independence is (at least rhetorically) highly valued. In practice, the relationship between independence and accountability is not straightforward. Although the doctrine does not consider them incom-patible and may even advocate their combination, the picture is more complex, and it is sufficient to note that accountability may undermine independence and impartiality through the shadow of sanctions. In reality, agencies are accountable to different kinds of forums, but when their accountability web becomes too crowded, this can create problems of duplication or cross-pressure. Furthermore, effective democratic control is not guaranteed because of a lack of public awareness about the role of agencies. However, agencies should not necessarily be incriminated for accountability gaps: they engage in accountability activities more actively than expected (namely, because they care about their reputations), but accountability forums are more passive than anticipated (among other reasons, because they trust agencies' reputations).

Knowing the role that media play as 'fire alarms', does accountability become stronger with the mediatization of politics and the advent of 'monitory' and 'audience' democracy, the effects of which are studied in Section 5? Governing actors – elected officials and increasingly top public managers – operate under the shadow of media criticism, and they seek to avoid or counteract the frequently negative bias in media coverage with presentational strategies of 'self-mediatization'. Of course, news management becomes more difficult with the growth of social media platforms, on which unchecked information easily becomes viral. This does not mean that monitory democracy faces no limitations. It is mainly front-stage politics that lends itself to media 'dramaturgy' and is put under the public 'microscope', so mediatization does not penetrate the whole policy process. Policy issues of low salience and measures that are too technical or lack a broad or tangible impact on people's lives do not score high in terms of newsworthiness, and many policy debates take place in narrow expert circles, and sometimes in remote arenas. Thus, they are not visible to the media who fail to perform their watchdog role. In other words, what frequently and increasingly occurs is a decoupling between the political spectacle and the reality of policy development, which may lead to errors in the attribution of responsibility. As mentioned previously, the consequence is a divorce between power wielding and public accountability.

It can be objected that this may be true for routine policy-making but not for critical situations: when perceptions that things went wrong dominate, policy-makers face more pressing demands for justification from official investigative bodies and strong claims for sanctions from opposition and stakeholder groups, with the media acting as catalysts. As disasters are difficult to accept, policy failure is an easy target for political exploitation, and postcrisis accountability may be harsh. Policy-makers need to react quickly and creatively to manage stressful situations and reassure public opinion. They are far from being powerless in their attempts to win battles of narratives by seeking to deflect the blame to 'lightning rods', so there is no guarantee that the gap between power and accountability decreases even in exceptional situations. However, policy-makers do not necessarily opt for strategies that are most efficacious for their survival, and the outcome of their attempts is uncertain and context dependent. The same can be said about the long-term consequences of postcrisis accountability regarding sanctions for failure and especially regarding the willingness and ability of policy-makers to learn from mishaps.

One finally needs to acknowledge that individuals' subjective perceptions and experiences of accountability pressure matter (Section 6). In particular, how actors react to accountability overloads (i.e., to pressure that they perceive as excessive) is a matter of debate. Advocates of principal–agent theory stress the risk of accountability leading to bad policy out of conformism but, at the same time, envisage that accountable actors can just simulate conformity by gaming the system. Such a conclusion is confirmed by public administration research, which also warns that public servants tend to shield themselves in the face of accountability pressure by adopting defensive behaviour such as formalism. Furthermore, too strong and too narrow an emphasis on accountability at the organizational level can cause prejudice to collective goal attainment.

The fine-grained picture of the microfoundations of accountable actors' cognitive and emotional states offered by experimental work in social and organizational psychology is most useful for the understanding of the complex processes of 'felt' accountability. This body of work confirms that supervision felt as abusive may lead to defensive bolstering and even risks backfiring; however, the outcome depends on a range of moderating factors, and there is evidence that accountability induces actors to become more self-reflective and self-critical. Overall, we learn that accountability has mostly positive effects on individual decision-making quality, contrasting, for example, with some gloomy predictions of dysfunctions that derive from the principal–agent framework. This relatively optimistic note may no longer be valid if accountability is in excess. Nevertheless, perceptions of this aspect inevitably vary, even when individuals are confronted with the same amount of accountability pressure, and responses to pressure are hard to predict. Moreover, if we begin to understand how public managers feel about their accountability obligations, we still know little about how politicians perceive them. Ironically, it is assumed that people generally behave as politicians when they are held accountable, but how real-world politicians feel and act in such situations has not been studied in detail. Not to mention, it may not be justified to infer behavioural patterns of collective actors, which are of interest to students of politics, from individual-level findings.

7.2 Accountability: Kaleidoscopic

A key conclusion is that political accountability is a truly kaleidoscopic phenomenon. It is not just that policy-making is complex, and therefore, accountability relations exist at multiple points and involve a great number of actors and forums that use diverse modes of interaction. Furthermore, accountability processes are multifaceted, potentially generating friction and entailing trade-offs, and the accountability of the individual and collective actors involved in policy-making processes is characterized by ambiguities in many respects:

- Elections seem to perform relatively well as an accountability mechanism, and they plausibly incentivise office-holders to be responsive to citizens' preferences. They probably do so because office-holders fear retrospective voting, although there may be a gap between their fears and citizens' actual behaviour. However, even though competitive elections are considered the primary channel of democratic accountability in representative government, confining the study of accountability to its electoral aspect leads to misperceptions. Moreover, although the coupling of vertical accountability to the citizenry with interinstitutional accountability forms is necessary, it may cause frictions.

- With regard to the latter, parliaments are unevenly able or willing to hold their government effectively accountable, so that lower *de facto* than *de jure* accountability rather unexpectedly results from forum passivity and not from agency drift. Even when parliamentary control is effective, it may come at the detriment of accountability to the public. By increasingly acting as instances of horizontal accountability, courts indirectly gain influence in the legislative process, as it is rational for policy-makers to anticipate their views. Such interference by the unelected has been criticized, but one should keep in mind that politicians may be able to limit it.

- Political control over the bureaucracy may have expanded, including paradoxically through participatory forms of accountability. Hence, the diffusion of the latter does not necessarily mean more democratic policy-making, but it remains uncertain if enhanced political control has become more effective. Political control is even openly seen as a threat to the impartiality and independence of the proliferating autonomous public agencies. However, this is not to say that technocratic power is unchecked, and accountability may even be overabundant. Top-level public managers and street-level employees are subject to various forms of cross-pressure resulting from conflicting accountability claims ('many eyes'), leading to dilemmas and disarray, as well as coping strategies and attempts to evade blame. Furthermore, some public agencies voluntarily strive to become accountable for reputational purposes. Thus, they may be more accountable in practice than *de jure*, but once an agency's reputation is established, accountability forums tend to trust it and remain inactive. The strategic use of accountability as a reputation-enhancing resource, intended to subsequently shield from overly invasive controls, is perhaps a more generalized mechanism in bureaucracies that has not yet been sufficiently studied.

- In the probably expanding collaborative forms of governance, public accountability competes with participants' peer accountability to their network partners. It is also *de facto* undermined because the allocation of responsibility becomes difficult ('many hands'), especially if collaborative networks are amorphous, informal and lack visibility, with the crucial rule-making actors remaining unseen to outsiders, even if unintentionally. When rule-making is 'coproduced' in hybrid partnerships and, even more so, outsourced to private bodies, then the exercise of power may even be divorced from *de jure* democratic accountability, which best epitomizes the role of accountability as a legitimacy-enhancing device.

- Relatedly, despite the mediatization of politics in a context of monitory or audience democracy and with the rising role of social media, it is above all front-stage politics, lending itself to media 'dramaturgy', that unfolds under the public 'microscope'. Significant activities of the policy-making process remain shielded from media scrutiny because they lack salience and newsworthiness and thus also lack relevance for the increasingly commercialized media agenda. Moreover, most journalists are insufficiently equipped for critical investigations. Hence, although the media are usually considered powerful 'fire alarms', they do not always adequately perform their role as accountability forums.

- The decoupling between the political spectacle and the reality of policy development, which undermines accountability's effectiveness, is likely to persist even in critical situations. On the one hand, policy failure is an easy target for political exploitation, so that postcrisis accountability may be harsh, and responses by policy-makers may prove inappropriate or insufficient to calm criticism. On the other hand, policy-makers are far from being powerless even in such critical episodes, for example, through their ability to deflect the blame, so that the long-term consequences of postcrisis accountability processes remain uncertain.

- Finally, we need to give credit to the quite nuanced conclusions of psychological research regarding accountability's impact on the feelings and the behaviour of individuals who are held accountable. This body of work shows that the reactions of individuals are shaped by a whole range of moderating factors, whereas studies of politics are, perhaps unduly, more assertive when they assume, for example, that politicians can decipher the preferences of accountability forums and adjust to them. The same applies to bureaucracy studies, which suggest that public managers and employees manage the stress caused by accountability pressure through various kinds of coping strategies. As the validity of such beliefs about policy-makers' attitudes and behavioural choices has been insufficiently tested until now, the study of accountability in politics would undoubtedly be improved by a careful incorporation of more evidence from social and organizational psychology.

This Element intended to show that cross-fertilization between various relatively insulated research communities is indeed indispensable to capture the prismatic nature of accountability. Studying policy-makers' accountability requires navigating arenas of governance that have varying properties, such as codification or visibility. It also requires looking at the role of institutions that we must not forget are populated by actors and, therefore, do not necessarily work as intended on paper, just as they do not always produce the expected results. An interactionist approach highlights the existence of complex accountability webs, involving various types of individual and collective actors in their roles as account-givers and account-holders, whose interdependence stems from different organizing principles that coexist, sometimes in a conflicting way, such as hierarchy, delegation, control, antagonism or cooperation. Furthermore, time matters, and accountability fluctuates between periods of routine and equilibrium and critical episodes of high dramatic intensity, in which vulnerabilities and defences come to light: reputations are called into question, but they can be used as a shield to protect oneself from criticism.

It is undoubtedly the variety of action repertoires and modes of interaction in accountability processes that is most striking. Actors seek to impose their narratives, enter into deliberation, struggle or negotiate. They are confronted with incentives and limitations and, therefore, reflect and calculate, but sometimes misperceive opportunities and constraints, as their prior beliefs and inadequate information generate noise. They are unevenly successful in building and damaging reputations, anticipating and managing expectations, taking preferences into account and reshaping them. They establish and challenge causalities, allocate and assume responsibilities, strategically learn to evade accountability and seek it voluntarily. Not less important than their cognitions are their emotions, including not only stress, fear and anger but also satisfaction and gratitude.

Finally, who should be held accountable, for what exactly, by whom, how and with what kind of consequences is often a matter of political controversy and sometimes not settled in normative debate. To give just a few illustrations of dilemmas and open questions: should actors that are not officially authorized to make collectively binding decisions be held politically accountable, and how can their contributions to policy-making be identified if they are unseen? How can one authoritatively assess to what extent constituencies are affected by policy? Which actors legitimately act as fire alarms and as account-holders? Should political accountability be primarily related to diffuse policy outcomes or to public goods delivered to particular target groups? What if responsiveness and democratic accountability to the citizenry collide with peer accountability and compliance with professional norms? Is the threat of sanctions indispensable to effective accountability, or depending on the purposes, should the approach be more educational than punitive? By highlighting core facets of the exercise and control of power, the study of policy-makers' accountability raises crucial questions on the quality of democratic government, the 'elephant in the corner' (Ingram and Schneider, 2016) of public policy theory.

References

Achen, C. H. and Bartels, L. M. (2017) *Democracy for Realists: Why Elections Do Not Produce Responsive Government*. Princeton: Princeton University Press.

Adam, C., Hurka, S., Knill, C. and Steinebach, Y. (2019) *Policy Accumulation and the Democratic Responsiveness Trap*. Cambridge: Cambridge University Press.

Aleksovska, M., Schillemans, T. and Grimmelikhuijsen, S. (2019) 'Lessons from five decades of experimental and behavioral research on accountability: A systematic literature review', *Journal of Behavioral Public Administration*, 2(2), pp. 1–18. https://doi.org/10.30636/jbpa.22.66.

Aleksovska, M., Schillemans, T. and Grimmelikhuijsen, S. (2022) 'Management of multiple accountabilities through setting priorities: Evidence from a cross-national conjoint experiment', *Public Administration Review*, 82(1), pp. 132–46. https://doi.org/10.1111/puar.13357.

Alon-Barkat, S. and Gilad, S. (2017) 'Compensating for poor performance with promotional symbols: Evidence from a survey experiment', *Journal of Public Administration Research and Theory*, 27(4), pp. 661–75. https://doi.org/10.1093/jopart/mux013.

Alter, K., Helfer, L. and Madsen, M. (eds.) (2018) *International Court Authority*. Oxford: Oxford University Press.

Anderson, C. J. (2000) 'Economic voting and political context: A comparative perspective', *Electoral Studies*, 19(2), pp. 151–70. https://doi.org/10.1016/S0261-3794(99)00045-1.

Anderson, C. J. (2007) 'The end of economic voting? Contingency dilemmas and the limits of democratic accountability', *Annual Review of Political Science*, 10, pp. 271–96.

Ansell, C. and Gash, A. (2008) 'Collaborative governance in theory and practice', *Journal of Public Administration Research and Theory*, 18(4), pp. 543–71. https://doi.org/10.1093/jopart/mum032.

Apaydin, F. and Jordana, J. (2020) 'Varying power configurations and the accountability of independent regulatory agencies', *International Review of Public Policy*, 2(3), pp. 342–57. https://doi.org/10.4000/irpp.1458.

Arceneaux, K. and Vander Wielen, R. J. (2017) *Taming Intuition: How Reflection Minimizes Partisan Reasoning and Promotes Democratic Accountability*. Cambridge: Cambridge University Press.

Auel, K. and Benz, A. (2005) 'The politics of adaptation: The Europeanisation of national parliamentary systems', *The Journal of Legislative Studies*, 11(3–4), pp. 372–93. https://doi.org/10.1080/13572330500273570.

Auel, K., Rozenberg, O. and Tacea, A. (2015) 'Fighting back? And, if so, how? Measuring parliamentary strength and activity in EU affairs', in Hefftler, C., Neuhold, C., Rozenberg, O. and Smith, J. (eds.) *The Palgrave Handbook of National Parliaments and the European Union*. London: Palgrave Macmillan, pp. 60–93.

Bach, T., Ruffing, E. and Yesilkagit, K. (2015) 'The differential empowering effects of Europeanization on the autonomy of national agencies', *Governance*, 28(3), pp. 285–304. https://doi.org/10.1111/gove.12087.

Bach, T., Van Thiel, S., Hammerschmid, G. and Steiner, R. (2017) 'Administrative tradition and management reforms: A comparison of agency chief executive accountability in four continental Rechtsstaat countries', *Public Management Review*, 19(6), pp. 765–84. https://doi.org/10.1080/14719037.2016.1210205.

Behn, R. D. (2001) *Rethinking Democratic Accountability*. Washington, DC: The Brookings Institution Press.

Benjamin, L. M. and Posner, P. L. (2018) 'Tax expenditures and accountability: The case of the ambivalent principals', *Journal of Public Administration Research and Theory*, 28(4), pp. 569–82. https://doi.org/10.1093/jopart/muy040.

Bertelli, A. M. (2016) 'Who are the policy workers, and what are they doing? Citizen's heuristics and democratic accountability in complex governance', *Public Performance & Management Review*, 40(2), pp. 208–34. https://doi.org/10.1080/15309576.2016.1180306.

Bertelli, A. M. and Busuioc, M. (2021) 'Reputation-sourced authority and the prospect of unchecked bureaucratic power', *Public Administration Review*, 81(1), pp. 38–48. https://doi.org/10.1111/puar.13281.

Bianculli, A., Jordana, J. and Fernández-i-Marín, X. (eds.) (2015) *Accountability and Regulatory Governance: Audiences, Controls and Responsibilities in the Politics of Regulation*. Basingstoke: Palgrave Macmillan.

Birkland, T. A. (2006) *Lessons of Disaster: Policy Change after Catastrophic Events*. Washington, DC: Georgetown University Press.

Blauberger, M. and Kelemen, R. D. (2017) 'Can courts rescue national democracy? Judicial safeguards against democratic backsliding in the EU', *Journal of European Public Policy*, 24(3), pp. 321–36. https://doi.org/10.1080/13501763.2016.1229357.

de Boer, T. (2022) 'Why do public agencies seek accountability? The role of audiences', *Public Administration*, early online view. https://doi.org/10.1111/padm.12859.

Boin, A., Brown, C. and Richardson, J. A. (2019) *Managing Hurricane Katrina: Lessons from a Megacrisis*. Baton Rouge: Louisiana State University Press.

Boin, A., McConnell, A. and 't Hart, P. (2008) 'Governing after crisis', in Boin, A., McConnell, A. and 't Hart, P. (eds.) *Governing after Crisis: The Politics of Investigation, Accountability and Learning.* Cambridge: Cambridge University Press, pp. 3–30.

Boin, A., 't Hart, P. and McConnell, A. (2008) 'Conclusions: The politics of crisis exploitation', in Boin, A., McConnell, A. and 't Hart, P. (eds.) *Governing after Crisis: The Politics of Investigation, Accountability and Learning.* Cambridge: Cambridge University Press, pp. 285–316.

Boin, A., 't Hart, P. and McConnell, A. (2009) 'Crisis exploitation: Political and policy impacts of framing contests', *Journal of European Public Policy*, 16(1), pp. 81–106. https://doi.org/10.1080/13501760802453221.

Boin, A., 't Hart, P., Stern, E. and Sundelius, B. (2005) *The Politics of Crisis Management: Public Leadership under Pressure.* Cambridge: Cambridge University Press.

Bovens, M. (2010) 'Two concepts of accountability: Accountability as a virtue and as a mechanism', *West European Politics*, 33(5), pp. 946–67. https://doi.org/10.1080/01402382.2010.486119.

Bovens, M., Curtin, D. and 't Hart, P. (2010) *The Real World of EU Accountability: What Deficit?* Oxford: Oxford University Press.

Bovens, M., Goodin, R. E. and Schillemans, T. (2014) 'Public accountability', in Bovens, M., Goodin, R. E. and Schillemans, T. (eds.) *The Oxford Handbook of Public Accountability.* Oxford: Oxford University Press, pp. 1–20.

Bovens, M. and Wille, A. (2021) 'Indexing watchdog accountability powers a framework for assessing the accountability capacity of independent oversight institutions', *Regulation & Governance*, 15(3), pp. 856–76. https://doi.org/10.1111/rego.12316.

Braithwaite, J. (1997) 'On speaking softly and carrying big sticks: Neglected dimensions of a republican separation of powers', *The University of Toronto Law Journal*, 47(3), pp. 305–61. https://doi.org/10.2307/825973.

Brandsma, G. J. and Moser, C. (2020) 'Accountability in a multi-jurisdictional order', in Scholten, M., Brenninkmeijer, A. and Strauss, B. (eds.) *Controlling EU Agencies: The Rule of Law in a Multi-jurisdictional Legal Order.* Cheltenham: Edward Elgar, pp. 60–79.

Brandsma, G. J. and Schillemans, T. (2013) 'The accountability cube: Measuring accountability', *Journal of Public Administration Research and Theory*, 23(4), pp. 953–75. https://doi.org/10.1093/jopart/mus034.

Breaux, D. M., Perrewé, P. L., Hall, A. T., Frink, D. D. and Hochwarter, W. A. (2008) 'Time to try a little tenderness? The detrimental effects of accountability when coupled with abusive supervision', *Journal of Leadership &*

Organizational Studies, 15(2), pp. 111–22. https://doi.org/10.1177/15480518 08321787.

Breunig, C., Grossman, E. and Hänni, M. (2022) 'Responsiveness and demo-cratic accountability: Observational evidence from an experiment in a mixed-member proportional system', *Legislative Studies Quarterly*, 47(1), pp. 79–94. https://doi.org/10.1111/lsq.12326.

Brouard, S. and Hönnige, C. (2017) 'Constitutional courts as veto players: Lessons from the United States, France and Germany', *European Journal of Political Research*, 56(3), pp. 529–52. https://doi.org/10.1111/1475-6765 .12192.

Brummel, L. (2021) 'Social accountability between consensus and confronta-tion: Developing a theoretical framework for societal accountability relation-ships of public sector organizations', *Administration & Society*, 53(7), pp. 1046–77. https://doi.org/10.1177/0095399720988529.

Busuioc, M. (2021) 'Accountable artificial intelligence: Holding algorithms to account', *Public Administration Review*, 81(5), pp. 825–36. https://doi .org/10.1111/puar.13293.

Busuioc, M. and Lodge, M. (2016) 'The reputational basis of public accountability', *Governance*, 29(2), pp. 247–63. https://doi.org/10.1111/ gove.12161.

Busuioc, M. and Lodge, M. (2017) 'Reputation and accountability relation-ships: Managing accountability expectations through reputation', *Public Administration Review*, 77(1), pp. 91–100. https://doi.org/10.1111/ puar.12612.

Cairney, P., Heikkila, T. and Wood, M. (2019) *Making Policy in a Complex World*. Cambridge: Cambridge University Press.

Caplan, B., Crampton, E., Grove, W. A. and Somin, I. (2013) 'Systematically biased beliefs about political influence: Evidence from the perceptions of political influence on policy outcomes survey', *PS: Political Science & Politics*, 46(4), pp. 760–7. https://doi.org/10.1017/S104 9096513001030.

Carpenter, D. and Krause, G. A. (2015) 'Transactional authority and bureau-cratic politics', *Journal of Public Administration Research and Theory*, 25 (1), pp. 5–25. https://doi.org/10.1093/jopart/muu012.

Carpenter, D. and Moss, D. A. (eds.) (2013) *Preventing Regulatory Capture: Special Interest Influence and How to Limit it*. Cambridge: Cambridge University Press.

Christensen, T. and Lægreid, P. (2015) 'Performance and accountability: A theoretical discussion and an empirical assessment', *Public Organization Review*, 15(2), pp. 207–25. https://doi.org/10.1007/s11115-013-0267-2.

Christensen, T. and Lægreid, P. (2017) 'Accountability relations in unsettled situations: Administrative reforms and crises', in Christensen, T. and Lægreid, P. (eds.) *The Routledge Handbook to Accountability and Welfare State Reforms in Europe*. Abingdon: Routledge, pp. 194–207.

Cichowski, R. (2013) 'Mobilisation, litigation and democratic governance', *Representation*, 49(3), pp. 321–32. https://doi.org/10.1080/00344893.2013.830484.

Cristofoli, D., Douglas, S., Torfing, J. and Trivellato, B. (2022) 'Having it all: Can collaborative governance be both legitimate and accountable?', *Public Management Review*, 24(5), pp. 704–28. https://doi.org/10.1080/14719037.2021.1960736.

Culpepper, P. D. (2010) *Quiet Politics and Business Power: Corporate Control in Europe and Japan*. Cambridge: Cambridge University Press.

Cutler, F. (2008) 'Whodunnit? Voters and responsibility in Canadian federalism', *Canadian Journal of Political Science*, 41(3), pp. 627–54.

Dalton, R. J., Cain, B. E. and Scarrow, S. E. (2003) 'Democratic publics and democratic institutions', in Cain, B. E., Dalton, R. J. and Scarrow, S. E. (eds.) *Democracy Transformed? Expanding Political Opportunities in Advanced Industrial Democracies*. Oxford: Oxford University Press, pp. 250–75.

Davis, J. H., Schoorman, F. D. and Donaldson, L. (1997) 'Toward a stewardship theory of management', *The Academy of Management Review*, 22(1), pp. 20–47. https://doi.org/10.2307/259223.

Denis, J.-L., Ferlie, E. and Gestel, N. V. (2015) 'Understanding hybridity in public organizations', *Public Administration*, 93(2), pp. 273–89. https://doi.org/10.1111/padm.12175.

Dimova, G. (2020) *Democracy Beyond Elections: Government Accountability in the Media Age*. Cham: Palgrave Macmillan.

Dommett, K. and Flinders, M. (2015) 'The centre strikes back: Meta-governance, delegation, and the core executive in the United Kingdom, 2010–14', *Public Administration*, 93(1), pp. 1–16. https://doi.org/10.1111/padm.12121.

Duch, R. M. and Stevenson, R. T. (2008) *The Economic Vote: How Political and Economic Institutions Condition Election Results*. Cambridge: Cambridge University Press.

Egeberg, M. and Trondal, J. (2009) 'National agencies in the European administrative space: Government driven, Commission driven or networked?', *Public Administration*, 87(4), pp. 779–90. https://doi.org/10.1111/j.1467-9299.2009.01779.x.

Emerson, K., Nabatchi, T. and Balogh, S. (2012) 'An integrative framework for collaborative governance', *Journal of Public Administration Research and Theory*, 22(1), pp. 1–29. https://doi.org/10.1093/jopart/mur011.

Eriksen, E. O. (2022) 'Strategies for reparing legitimacy deficits', in Eriksen, E. O. (ed.) *The Accountability of Expertise: Making the Un-elected Safe for Democracy*. Abingdon: Routledge, pp. 14–33.

Esser, F. and Strömbäck, J. (eds.) (2014) *Mediatization of Politics: Understanding the Transformation of Western Democracies*. Basingstoke: Palgrave Macmillan.

Fabbrini, S. (2015) *Which European Union? Europe after the Euro Crisis*. Cambridge: Cambridge University Press.

Fawcett, P., Flinders, M. V., Hay, C. and Wood, M. (eds.) (2017) *Anti-politics, Depoliticization, and Governance*. Oxford: Oxford University Press.

Finer, H. (1941) 'Administrative responsibility in democratic government', *Public Administration Review*, 1(4), pp. 335–50. https://doi.org/10.2307/972907.

Flinders, M. (2012) *Defending Politics: Why Democracy Matters in the 21st Century*. Oxford: Oxford University Press.

Fortunato, D., Martin, L. W. and Vanberg, G. (2019) 'Committee chairs and legislative review in parliamentary democracies', *British Journal of Political Science*, 49(2), pp. 785–97. https://doi.org/10.1017/S0007123416000673.

Fossheim, K. (2022) 'How can non-elected representatives secure democratic representation?', *Policy & Politics*, 50(2), pp. 243–60. https://doi.org/10.1332/030557321X16371011677734.

Friedrich, C. J. (1937) *Constitutional Government and Politics*. New York: Harper.

Friedrich, C. J. (1940) 'Public policy and the nature of administrative responsibility', in Friedrich, C. J. and Mason, E. S. (eds.) *Public Policy*. Cambridge, MA: Harvard University Press, pp. 3–24.

Garoupa, N. and Ginsburg, T. (2015) *Judicial Reputation: A Comparative Study*. Chicago: Chicago University Press.

Gasper, J. T. and Reeves, A. (2011) 'Make it rain? Retrospection and the attentive electorate in the context of natural disasters', *American Journal of Political Science*, 55(2), pp. 340–55. https://doi.org/10.1111/j.1540-5907.2010.00503.x.

Gersen, J. E. and Stephenson, M. C. (2014) 'Over-accountability', *Journal of Legal Analysis*, 6(2), pp. 185–243. https://doi.org/10.1093/jla/lau008.

Ginsburg, T. (2008) 'The global spread of constitutional review', in Caldeira, G. A., Kelemen, R. D. and Whittington, K. E. (eds.) *The Oxford Handbook of Law and Politics*. Oxford: Oxford University Press, pp. 81–98.

Girth, A. M. (2014) 'A closer look at contract accountability: Exploring the determinants of sanctions for unsatisfactory contract performance', *Journal of Public Administration Research and Theory*, 24(2), pp. 317–48. https://doi.org/10.1093/jopart/mus033.

Gomez, B. T. and Wilson, J. M. (2008) 'Political sophistication and attributions of blame in the wake of hurricane Katrina', *Publius: The Journal of Federalism*, 38(4), pp. 633–50. https://doi.org/10.1093/publius/pjn016.

Goodhart, M. (2011) 'Democratic accountability in global politics: Norms, not agents', *The Journal of Politics*, 73(1), pp. 45–60. https://doi.org/10.1017/S002238161000085X.

Goodin, R. E. (2003) *Reflective Democracy*. Oxford: Oxford University Press.

Goodin, R. E. (2007) 'Enfranchising all affected interests, and its alternatives', *Philosophy & Public Affairs*, 35(1), pp. 40–68. https://doi.org/10.1111/j.1088-4963.2007.00098.x.

Grigorescu, A. (2015) *Democratic Intergovernmental Organizations? Normative Pressures and Decision-Making Rules*. Cambridge: Cambridge University Press.

Grossman, E. (2022) 'Media and policy making in the digital age', *Annual Review of Political Science*, 25(1), pp. 443–61. https://doi.org/10.1146/annurev-polisci-051120-103422.

Grube, D. C. (2019) *Megaphone Bureaucracy: Speaking Truth to Power in the Age of the New Normal*. Princeton: Princeton University Press.

Hajer, M. A. (2009) *Authoritative Governance: Policy Making in the Age of Mediatization*. Oxford: Oxford University Press.

Halachmi, A. (2014) 'Accountability overloads', in Bovens, M., Goodin, R. E. and Schillemans, T. (eds.) *The Oxford Handbook of Public Accountability*. Oxford: Oxford University Press, pp. 560–73.

Hall, A. T., Frink, D. D. and Buckley, M. R. (2017) 'An accountability account: A review and synthesis of the theoretical and empirical research on felt accountability', *Journal of Organizational Behavior*, 38(2), pp. 204–24. https://doi.org/10.1002/job.2052.

Hameleers, M., Bos, L. and de Vreese, C. H. (2019) 'Shoot the messenger? The media's role in framing populist attributions of blame', *Journalism*, 20(9), pp. 1145–64. https://doi.org/10.1177/1464884917698170.

Han, Y. and Robertson, P. (2021) 'Public employee accountability: An empirical examination of a nomological network', *Public Performance & Management Review*, 44(3), pp. 494-522. https://doi.org/10.1080/15309576.2020.1803092.

Hanretty, C. and Koop, C. (2013) 'Shall the law set them free? The formal and actual independence of regulatory agencies', *Regulation & Governance*, 7(2), pp. 195–214. https://doi.org/10.1111/j.1748-5991.2012.01156.x.

Hasler, K., Küebler, D. and Marcinkowksi, F. (2016) 'Over-responsibilised and over-blamed: Elected actors in media reporting on network governance. A comparative analysis in eight European metropolitan areas', *Policy & Politics*, 44(1), pp. 135–52. https://doi.org/10.1332/030557315X14434668993301.

Hassenteufel, P. and Genieys, W. (2021) 'The Programmatic Action Framework: An empirical assessment', *European Policy Analysis*, 7(S1), pp. 28–47. https://doi.org/10.1002/epa2.1088.

Hawkins, D. G. and Jacoby, W. (2006) 'How agents matter', in Hawkins, D. G., Lake, D. A., Nielson, D. and Tierney, M. J. (eds.) *Delegation and Agency in International Organizations*. Cambridge: Cambridge University Press, pp. 199–228.

Healy, A. J., Malhotra, N. and Mo, C. H. (2010) 'Irrelevant events affect voters' evaluations of government performance', *Proceedings of the National Academy of Sciences*, 107(29), pp. 12804–9.

Hellwig, T. and Samuels, D. (2008) 'Electoral accountability and the variety of democratic regimes', *British Journal of Political Science*, 38(1), pp. 65–90. https://doi.org/10.1017/S0007123408000045.

Hill, C. J. and Lynn, L. E., Jr. (2005) 'Is hierarchical governance in decline? Evidence from empirical research', *Journal of Public Administration Research and Theory*, 15(2), pp. 173–95. https://doi.org/10.1093/jopart/mui011.

Hinterleitner, M. (2017) 'Reconciling perspectives on blame avoidance behaviour', *Political Studies Review*, 15(2), pp. 243–54. https://doi.org/10.1111/1478-9302.12099.

Hinterleitner, M. (2020) *Policy Controversies and Political Blame Games*. Cambridge: Cambridge University Press.

Hirschl, R. (2008) 'The judicialization of mega-politics and the rise of political courts', *Annual Review of Political Science*, 11(1), pp. 93–118. https://doi.org/10.1146/annurev.polisci.11.053006.183906.

Hirschl, R. (2013) 'Epilogue: Courts and democracy between ideals and realities', *Representation*, 49(3), pp. 361–73. https://doi.org/10.1080/00344893.2013.830487.

Hirschmann, G. (2020) *Accountability in Global Governance: Pluralist Accountability in Global Governance*. Oxford: Oxford University Press.

Hobolt, S., Tilley, J. and Banducci, S. (2013) 'Clarity of responsibility: How government cohesion conditions performance voting', *European Journal of Political Research*, 52(2), pp. 164–87. https://doi.org/10.1111/j.1475-6765.2012.02072.x.

Hobolt, S. B. and Tilley, J. (2014) *Blaming Europe? Responsibility without Accountability in the European Union*. Oxford: Oxford University Press.

Hochwarter, W. A., Ferris, G. R., Gavin, M. B. et al. (2007) 'Political skill as neutralizer of felt accountability – job tension effects on job performance ratings: A longitudinal investigation', *Organizational Behavior and Human Decision Processes*, 102(2), pp. 226–39. https://doi.org/10.1016/j.obhdp.2006.09.003.

Hohendorf, L., Saalfeld, T. and Sieberer, U. (2021) 'Veto power fosters coopera-tive behaviour: Institutional incentives and government-opposition voting in the German Bundestag', *West European Politics*, 44(4), pp. 921–45. https://doi.org/10.1080/01402382.2020.1739868.

Hood, C. (2010) *The Blame Game: Spin, Bureaucracy, and Self-Preservation in Government*. Princeton: Princeton University Press.

Hood, C. (2015) 'Blame avoidance and accountability: Positive, negative, or neutral?', in Dubnick, M. A. and Frederickson, H. G. (eds.) *Accountable Governance: Problems and Promises*. Abingdon: Routledge, pp. 167–79.

Hood, C., James, O., Jones, G., Scott, C. and Travers, T. (1999) *Regulation Inside Government: Waste-Watchers, Quality Police, and Sleazebusters*. Oxford: Oxford University Press.

Hood, C., Jennings, W. and Copeland, P. (2016) 'Blame avoidance in compara-tive perspective: Reactivity, staged retreat and efficacy', *Public Administration*, 94(2), pp. 542–62. https://doi.org/10.1111/padm.12235.

Hood, C. and Lodge, M. (2006) *The Politics of Public Service Bargains: Reward, Competency, Loyalty – and Blame*. Oxford: Oxford University Press.

Howlett, M., Ramesh, M. and Perl, A. (2009) *Studying Public Policy: Policy Cycles & Policy Subsystems*. Oxford: Oxford University Press.

Huber, J. D. and Shipan, C. R. (2002) *Deliberate Discretion? The Institutional Foundations of Bureaucratic Autonomy*. Cambridge: Cambridge University Press.

Hupe, P. and Edwards, A. (2012) 'The accountability of power: Democracy and governance in modern times', *European Political Science Review*, 4(2), pp. 177–94. https://doi.org/10.1017/S1755773911000154.

Hupe, P. and Hill, M. (2007) 'Street-level bureaucracy and public accountability', *Public Administration*, 85(2), pp. 279–99. https://doi.org/10.1111/j.1467-9299.2007.00650.x.

Immergut, E. M. (1992) *Health Politics: Interests and Institutions in Western Europe*. Cambridge: Cambridge University Press.

Ingold, K. and Varone, F. (2012) 'Treating policy brokers seriously: Evidence from the climate policy', *Journal of Public Administration Research and Theory*, 22(2), pp. 319–46. https://doi.org/10.1093/jopart/mur035.

Ingram, H. and Schneider, A. (2016) 'Conclusion: Public policy theory and democracy: The elephant in the corner', in Peters, B. G. and Zittoun, P. (eds.) *Contemporary Policy Approaches, Theories, Controversies, and Perspectives*. London: Palgrave Macmillan, pp. 175–200.

Iyengar, S. (1991) *Is Anyone Responsible? How Television Frames Political Issues*. Chicago: Chicago University Press.

Jacobs, A. M. (2011) *Governing for the Long Term: Democracy and the Politics of Investment*. Cambridge: Cambridge University Press.

Jacobs, S. and Schillemans, T. (2016) 'Media and public accountability: Typology and exploration', *Policy & Politics*, 44(1), pp. 23–40. https://doi .org/10.1332/030557315X14431855320366.

James, O., Jilke, S., Petersen, C. and Van de Walle, S. (2016) 'Citizens' blame of politicians for public service failure: Experimental evidence about blame reduction through delegation and contracting', *Public Administration Review*, 76(1), pp. 83–93. https://doi.org/10.1111/puar.12471.

Jann, W. (2016) 'Accountability, performance and legitimacy in the welfare state', in Christensen, T. and Lægreid, P. (eds.) *The Routledge Handbook to Accountability and Welfare State Reforms in Europe*. Abingdon: Routledge, pp. 31–44.

Jantz, B., Klenk, T., Larsen, F. and Wiggan, J. (2018) 'Marketization and varieties of accountability relationships in employment services: Comparing Denmark, Germany, and Great Britain', *Administration & Society*, 50(3), pp. 321–45. https://doi.org/10.1177/0095399715581622.

Jordana, J. (2017) 'Accountability challenges in the governance of infrastructure', in Wegrich, K., Kostka, G. and Hammerschmid, G. (eds.) *The Governance of Infrastructure*. Oxford: Oxford University Press, pp. 43–62.

Jordana, J., Fernández-i-Marín, X. and Bianculli, A. C. (2018) 'Agency proliferation and the globalization of the regulatory state: Introducing a data set on the institutional features of regulatory agencies', *Regulation & Governance*, 12(4), pp. 524–40. https://doi.org/10.1111/rego.12189.

Kam, C., Bertelli, A. M. and Held, A. (2020) 'The electoral system, the party system and accountability in parliamentary government', *American Political Science Review*, 114(3), pp. 744–60. https://doi.org/10.1017/ S0003055420000143.

Karsten, N. (2015) 'Scrutinize me, please! The drivers, manifestations and implications of accountability-seeking behaviour', *Public Administration*, 93(3), pp. 684–99. https://doi.org/10.1111/padm.12164.

Keane, J. (2009) *The Life and Death of Democracy*. New York: W. W. Norton.

Kennedy, J., Sayers, A. and Alcantara, C. (2022) 'Does federalism prevent democratic accountability? Assigning responsibility for rates of COVID-19 testing', *Political Studies Review*, 20(1), pp. 158–65. https://doi.org/10.1177/ 14789299211001690.

Klenk, T. and Cohen, N. (2019) 'Dealing with hybridization in street-level bureaucracy research', in Hupe, P. (ed.) *Research Handbook on Street-Level Bureaucracy*. Cheltenham: Edgar Elgar, pp. 142–56.

Knight, J. and Schwartzberg, M. (2020) 'Institutional bargaining for democratic theorists (or how we learned to stop worrying and love haggling)', *Annual Review of Political Science*, 23(1), pp. 259–76. https://doi.org/10.1146/annurev-polisci-060118-102113.

Koenig-Archibugi, M. (2017) 'Accountability', in Kogan, J. K., Hurd, I. and Johnstone, I. (eds.) *The Oxford Handbook of International Organizations*. Oxford: Oxford University Press, online version. https://doi.org/10.1093/law/9780199672202.003.0054.

Koliba, C. J., Mills, R. M. and Zia, A. (2011) 'Accountability in governance networks: An assessment of public, private, and nonprofit emergency management practices following hurricane Katrina', *Public Administration Review*, 71(2), pp. 210–20. https://doi.org/10.1111/j.1540-6210.2011.02332.x.

König, P.D., Felfeli, J., Achtziger, A. and Wenzelburger, G. (2022) 'The importance of effectiveness versus transparency and stakeholder involvement in citizens' perception of public sector algorithms', *Public Management Review*, early online view. https://doi.org/10.1080/14719037.2022.2144938.

Koop, C. (2011) 'Explaining the accountability of independent agencies: The importance of political salience', *Journal of Public Policy*, 31(2), pp. 209–34. https://doi.org/10.1017/S0143814X11000080.

Koop, C. (2014) 'Theorizing and explaining voluntary accountability', *Public Administration*, 92(3), pp. 565–81. https://doi.org/10.1111/padm.12058.

Koop, C. and Lodge, M. (2020) 'British economic regulators in an age of politicisation: From the responsible to the responsive regulatory state?', *Journal of European Public Policy*, 27(11), pp. 1612–35. https://doi.org/10.1080/13501763.2020.1817127.

Koppell, J. G. (2005) 'Pathologies of accountability: ICANN and the challenge of "multiple accountabilities disorder"', *Public Administration Review*, 65(1), pp. 94–108. https://doi.org/10.1111/j.1540-6210.2005.00434.x.

Kratochwil, F. (2008) 'Has the "rule of law" become a "rule of lawyers"? An inquiry into the use and abuse of an ancient topos in contemporary debates', in Palombella, G. and Walker, N. (eds.) *Relocating the Rule of Law*. Oxford: Hart, pp. 171–96.

Kriner, D. L. and Schickler, E. (2017) *Investigating the President: Congressional Checks on Presidential Power*. Princeton: Princeton University Press.

Kuipers, S. and Brändström, A. (2020) 'Accountability and blame avoidance after crises', in Thompson, W. R. (ed.) *Oxford Research Encyclopedia of Politics*. https://doi.org/10.1093/acrefore/9780190228637.013.1498.

Kuipers, S. and 't Hart, P. (2014) 'Accounting for crises', in Bovens, M., Goodin, R. E. and Schillemans, T. (eds.) *The Oxford Handbook of Public Accountability*. Oxford: Oxford University Press, pp.589–602.

Kuyper, J. W. and Squatrito, T. (2017) 'International courts and global democratic values: Participation, accountability, and justification', *Review of International Studies*, 43(1), pp. 152–76. https://doi.org/10.1017/S0260 210516000218.

Lægreid, P. (2014) 'Accountability and new public management', in Bovens, M., Goodin, R. E. and Schillemans, T. (eds.) *The Oxford Handbook of Public Accountability*. Oxford: Oxford University Press, pp. 324–38.

Langvatn, S. A. and Holst, C. (2022) 'Expert accountability: What does it mean, why is it challenging – and is it what we need?', *Constellations*, early online view. https://doi.org/10.1111/1467-8675.12649.

León, S. (2018) 'Muddling up political systems? When regionalization blurs democracy: Decentralization and attribution of responsibility', *Journal of Common Market Studies*, 56(3), pp. 706–16. https://doi.org/10.1111/jcms.12723.

León, S., Jurado, I. and Madariaga, A. G. (2018) 'Passing the buck? Responsibility attribution and cognitive bias in multilevel democracies', *West European Politics*, 41(3), pp. 660–82. https://doi.org/10.1080/01402382.2017.1405325.

Lerner, J. and Tetlock, P. (1999) 'Accounting for the effects of accountability', *Psychological Bulletin*, 125(2), pp. 255–75. https://doi.org/10.1037/0033-2909.125.2.255.

Li, Y., Qin, X. and Koppenjan, J. (2022) 'Accountability through public participation? Experiences from the ten-thousand-citizen review in Nanjing, China', *Journal of Public Policy*, 42(1), pp. 43–62. https://doi.org/10.1017/S0143814X21000027.

Liston-Heyes, C. and Juillet, L. (2022) 'What has become of the audit explosion? Analysing trends in oversight activities in the Canadian government', *Public Administration*, 100(4), pp. 1073-1090. https://doi.org/10.1111/padm.12793.

Maestas, C. D., Atkeson, L. R., Croom, T. and Bryant, L. A. (2008) 'Shifting the blame: Federalism, media, and public assignment of blame following hurricane Katrina', *Publius: The Journal of Federalism*, 38(4), pp. 609–32. https://doi.org/10.1093/publius/pjn021.

Maggetti, M. and Papadopoulos, Y. (2022) 'Happily unaccountable? Perceptions of accountability by public managers', *Public Policy and Administration,* early online view. https://doi.org/10.1177/09520767221074487.

Majone, G. (2001) 'Two logics of delegation: Agency and fiduciary relations in EU governance',*European Union Politics*, 2(1), pp. 103–22. https://doi.org/10.1177/1465116501002001005.

Manin, B. (1997) *The Principles of Representative Government*. Cambridge: Cambridge University Press.

Mansbridge, J. (2003) 'Rethinking representation', *American Political Science Review*, 97(4), pp. 515–28. https://doi.org/10.1017/S0003055403000856.

Maor, M. (2012) 'Policy overreaction', *Journal of Public Policy*, 32(3), pp. 231–59. https://doi.org/10.1017/S0143814X1200013X.

Maravall, J. M. and Sanchez-Cuenca, I. (2009) *Controlling Governments: Voters, Institutions, and Accountability*. Cambridge: Cambridge University Press.

March, J. G. and Olsen, J. P. (2013) 'The logic of appropriateness', in Goodin, R. E. (ed.) *The Oxford Handbook of Political Science*. Oxford: Oxford University Press, online version. https://doi.org/10.1093/oxfordhb/9780199604456.013.0024.

Maricut-Akbik, A. (2020) 'Contesting the European Central Bank in banking supervision: Accountability in practice at the European Parliament', *Journal of Common Market Studies*, 58(5), pp. 1199–214. https://doi.org/10.1111/jcms.13024.

Markakis, M. (2020) *Accountability in the Economic and Monetary Union: Foundations, Policy, and Governance*. Oxford: Oxford University Press.

Marvel, J. D. and Girth, A. M. (2016) 'Citizen attributions of blame in third-party governance', *Public Administration Review*, 76(1), pp. 96–108. https://doi.org/10.1111/puar.12474.

Mashaw, J. L. (2006) 'Accountability and institutional design: Some thoughts on the grammar of governance', in Dowdle, M. W. (ed.) *Public Accountability: Designs, Dilemmas and Experiences*. Cambridge: Cambridge University Press, pp. 115–56.

Matthieß, T. (2020) 'Retrospective pledge voting: A comparative study of the electoral consequences of government parties' pledge fulfilment', *European Journal of Political Research*, 59(4), pp. 774–96. https://doi.org/10.1111/1475-6765.12377.

McCubbins, M. D. and Schwartz, T. (1984) 'Congressional oversight overlooked: Police patrols versus fire alarms', *American Journal of Political Science*, 28(1), pp. 165–79. https://doi.org/10.2307/2110792.

McGraw, K. M. and Dolan, T. M. (2007) 'Personifying the state: Consequences for attitude formation', *Political Psychology*, 28(3), pp. 299–327.

Mechkova, V., Lührmann, A. and Lindberg, S. I. (2019) 'The accountability sequence: From de-jure to de-facto constraints on governments', *Studies in Comparative International Development*, 54(1), pp. 40–70. https://doi.org/10.1007/s12116-018-9262-5.

Merkel, W. (2004) 'Embedded and defective democracies', *Democratization*, 11(5), pp. 33–58. https://doi.org/10.1080/13510340412331304598.

Miller, G. J. (2005) 'The political evolution of principal-agent models', *Annual Review of Political Science*, 8(1), pp. 203–25. https://doi.org/10.1146/annurev.polisci.8.082103.104840.

Miller, G. J. and Whitford, A. B. (2016) *Above Politics: Bureaucratic Discretion and Credible Commitment*. Cambridge: Cambridge University Press.

Moe, T. M. (1984) 'The new economics of organization', *American Journal of Political Science*, 28(4), pp. 739–77. https://doi.org/10.2307/2110997.

Montanaro, L. (2017) *Who Elected Oxfam? A Democratic Defense of Self-Appointed Representatives*. Cambridge: Cambridge University Press.

Mortensen, P. B. (2016) 'Agencification and blame shifting: Evaluating a neglected side of public sector reforms', *Public Administration*, 94(3), pp. 630–46. https://doi.org/10.1111/padm.12243.

Moynihan, D. P. (2012) 'Extra-network organizational reputation and blame avoidance in networks: The hurricane Katrina example', *Governance*, 25(4), pp. 567–88. https://doi.org/10.1111/j.1468-0491.2012.01593.x.

Mulgan, R. (2000a) '"Accountability": An ever-expanding concept?', *Public Administration*, 78(3), pp. 555–73. https://doi.org/10.1111/1467-9299.00218.

Mulgan, R. (2000b) 'Comparing accountability in the public and private sectors', *Australian Journal of Public Administration*, 59(1), pp. 87–97. https://doi.org/10.1111/1467-8500.00142.

Nguyen, L., Rawat, P. and Morris, J. C. (2020) 'Accountability in the context of private policy implementation', in Sullivan, H., Dickinson, H. and Henderson, H. (eds.) *The Palgrave Handbook of the Public Servant*. Cham: Springer International, pp. 631–49.

Nielsen, P. A. and Moynihan, D. P. (2017) 'How do politicians attribute bureaucratic responsibility for performance? Negativity bias and interest group advocacy', *Journal of Public Administration Research and Theory*, 27(2), pp. 269–83. https://doi.org/10.1093/jopart/muw060.

O'Donnell, G. A. (1998) 'Horizontal accountability in new democracies', *Journal of Democracy*, 9(3), pp. 112–26. https://doi.org/10.1353/jod.1998.0051.

Olsen, J. P. (2015) 'Democratic order, autonomy, and accountability', *Governance*, 28(4), pp. 425–40. https://doi.org/10.1111/gove.12158.

Olsen, J. P. (2017) *Democratic Accountability, Political Order, and Change: Exploring Accountability Processes in an Era of European Transformation*. Oxford: Oxford University Press.

Opperhuizen, A. E., Klijn, E. H. and Schouten, K. (2020) 'How do media, political and regulatory agendas influence one another in high risk policy issues?', *Policy & Politics*, 48(3), pp. 461–83. https://doi.org/10.1332/030557319X15734252420020.

Ossege, C. (2012) 'Accountability – are we better off without it?', *Public Management Review*, 14(5), pp. 585–607. https://doi.org/10.1080/14719037.2011.642567.

Overman, S., Genugten, M. V. and Thiel, S. V. (2015) 'Accountability after structural disaggregation: Comparing agency accountability arrangements', *Public Administration*, 93(4), pp. 1102–20. https://doi.org/10.1111/padm.12185.

Overman, S. and Schillemans, T. (2022) 'Toward a public administration theory of felt accountability', *Public Administration Review*, 82(1), pp. 12–22. https://doi.org/10.1111/puar.13417.

Overman, S., Schillemans, T. and Grimmelikhuijsen, S. (2021) 'A validated measurement for felt relational accountability in the public sector: Gauging the account holder's legitimacy and expertise', *Public Management Review*, 23(12), pp. 1748–67. https://doi.org/10.1080/14719037.2020.1751254.

Papadopoulos, Y. (2007) 'Problems of democratic accountability in network and multilevel governance', *European Law Journal*, 13(4), pp. 469–86. https://doi.org/10.1111/j.1468-0386.2007.00379.x.

Papadopoulos, Y. (2012) '"Daring to be a Daniel": How much does it contribute to a "more fine-grained understanding" of pathologies of accountability?', *Administration & Society*, 44(2), pp. 238–52. https://doi.org/10.1177/0095399712448004.

Papadopoulos, Y. (2013) *Democracy in Crisis? Politics, Governance and Policy*. Basingstoke: Palgrave Macmillan.

Pelizzo, R. and Stapenhurst, F. (2014) *Government Accountability and Legislative Oversight*. Abingdon: Routledge.

Peters, B. G. (2014) 'Accountability in public administration', in Bovens, M., Goodin, R. E. and Schillemans, T. (eds.) *The Oxford Handbook of Public Accountability*. Oxford: Oxford University Press, pp. 211–25.

Peters, B. G. (2017) 'What is so wicked about wicked problems? A conceptual analysis and a research program', *Policy and Society*, 36(3), pp. 385–96. https://doi.org/10.1080/14494035.2017.1361633.

Peters, B. G. (2021) *Administrative Traditions: Understanding the Roots of Contemporary Administrative Behavior*. Oxford: Oxford University Press.

Peters, B. G. and Nagel, M. L. (2020) *Zombie Ideas: Why Failed Policy Ideas Persist*. Cambridge: Cambridge University Press.

Philp, M. (2009) 'Delimiting democratic accountability', *Political Studies*, 57(1), pp. 28–53. https://doi.org/10.1111/j.1467-9248.2008.00720.x.

Piatak, J., Romzek, B., LeRoux, K. and Johnston, J. (2018) 'Managing goal conflict in public service delivery networks: Does accountability move up and down, or side to side?', *Public Performance & Management Review*, 41(1), pp. 152–76. https://doi.org/10.1080/15309576.2017.1400993.

Pierson, P. (1994) *Dismantling the Welfare State? Reagan, Thatcher and the Politics of Retrenchment*. Cambridge: Cambridge University Press.

Plattner, M. F., Diamond, L. and Walker, C. (eds.) (2016) *Authoritarianism Goes Global: The Challenge to Democracy*. Baltimore: Johns Hopkins University Press.

Poguntke, T. and Webb, P. (eds.) (2005) *The Presidentialization of Politics: A Comparative Study of Modern Democracies*. Oxford: Oxford University Press.

Pollitt, C. (2015) 'Performance blight and the tyranny of light? Accountability in advanced performance management regimes', in Dubnick, M. J. and Frederickson, H. G. (eds.) *Accountable Governance: Problems and Promises*. Abingdon: Routledge, pp. 81–97.

Pollitt, C. and Bouckaert, G. (2017) *Public Management Reform: A Comparative Analysis – Into the Age of Austerity*. Oxford: Oxford University Press.

Pollitt, C. and Hupe, P. (2011) 'Talking about government: The role of magic concepts', *Public Management Review*, 13(5), pp. 641–58. https://doi.org/10.1080/14719037.2010.532963.

Posner, E. A. and Vermeule, A. (2011) *The Executive Unbound: After the Madisonian Republic*. New York: Oxford University Press.

Potter, R. A. (2019) *Bending the Rules: Procedural Politicking in the Bureaucracy*. Chicago: University of Chicago Press.

Powell, G. B. and Whitten, G. D. (1993) 'A cross-national analysis of economic voting: Taking account of the political context', *American Journal of Political Science*, 37(2), pp. 391–414. https://doi.org/10.2307/2111378.

Power, M. (1999) *The Audit Society: Rituals of Verification*. Oxford: Oxford University Press.

Rasmussen, A., Reher, S. and Toshkov, D. (2019) 'The opinion-policy nexus in Europe and the role of political institutions', *European Journal of Political Research*, 58(2), pp. 412–34. https://doi.org/10.1111/1475-6765.12286.

Raunio, T. and Hix, S. (2000) 'Backbenchers learn to fight back: European integration and parliamentary government', *West European Politics*, 23(4), pp. 142–68. https://doi.org/10.1080/01402380008425404.

Rock, E. (2020) *Measuring Accountability in Public Governance Regimes*. Cambridge: Cambridge University Press.

Romzek, B. S. and Dubnick, M. J. (1987) 'Accountability in the public sector: Lessons from the challenger tragedy', *Public Administration Review*, 47(3), pp. 227–38. https://doi.org/10.2307/975901.

Romzek, B. S. and Ingraham, P. W. (2000) 'Cross pressures of accountability: Initiative, command, and failure in the Ron Brown plane crash', *Public*

Administration Review, 60(3), pp. 240–53. https://doi.org/10.1111/0033-3352.00084.

Romzek, B. S., LeRoux, K. and Blackmar, J. M. (2012) 'A preliminary theory of informal accountability among network organizational actors', *Public Administration Review*, 72(3), pp. 442–53. https://doi.org/10.1111/j.1540-6210.2011.02547.x.

Romzek, B., LeRoux, K., Johnston, J., Kempf, R. J. and Piatak, J. S. (2014) 'Informal accountability in multisector service delivery collaborations', *Journal of Public Administration Research and Theory*, 24(4), pp. 813–42. https://doi.org/10.1093/jopart/mut027.

Royed, T. J., Leyden, K. M. and Borrelli, S. A. (2000) 'Is "clarity of responsibility" important for economic voting? Revisiting Powell and Whitten's hypothesis', *British Journal of Political Science*, 30(4), pp. 669–85.

Rubenstein, J. (2007) 'Accountability in an unequal world', *Journal of Politics*, 69(3), pp. 616–32. https://doi.org/10.1111/j.1468-2508.2007.00563.x.

Rudalevige, A. (2021) *By Executive Order: Bureaucratic Management and the Limits of Presidential Power*. Princeton: Princeton University Press.

Sager, F., Thomann, E. and Hupe, P. (2020) 'Accountability of public servants at the street level', in Sullivan, H., Dickinson, H. and Henderson, H. (eds.) *The Palgrave Handbook of the Public Servant*. Cham: Springer International, pp. 801–18.

Savoie, D. (2008) *Court Government and the Collapse of Accountability in Canada and the United Kingdom*. Toronto: University of Toronto Press.

Schillemans, T. (2010) 'Redundant accountability: The joint impact of horizontal and vertical accountability on autonomous agencies', *Public Administration Quarterly*, 34(3), pp. 300–37.

Schillemans, T. (2011) 'Does horizontal accountability work? Evaluating potential remedies for the accountability deficit of agencies', *Administration & Society*, 43(4), pp. 387–416. https://doi.org/10.1177/0095399711412931.

Schillemans, T. (2012) *Mediatization of Public Services: How Organizations Adapt to News Media*. Frankfurt: Peter Lang.

Schillemans, T. (2015) 'Managing public accountability: How public managers manage public accountability', *International Journal of Public Administration*, 38(6), pp. 433–41. https://doi.org/10.1080/01900692.2014.949738.

Schillemans, T. (2016) 'Calibrating public sector accountability: Translating experimental findings to public sector accountability', *Public Management Review*, 18(9), pp. 1400–20. https://doi.org/10.1080/14719037.2015.1112423.

Schillemans, T. and Bovens, M. (2015) 'The challenge of multiple accountability: Does redundancy lead to overload?', in Dubnick, M. J. and Frederickson, H. G. (eds.) *Accountable Governance: Problems and Promises*. Abingdon: Routledge, pp. 3–21.

Schillemans, T. and Busuioc, M. (2015) 'Predicting public sector accountability: From agency drift to forum drift', *Journal of Public Administration Research and Theory*, 25(1), pp. 191–215. https://doi.org/10.1093/jopart/muu024.

Schillemans, T., Karlsen, R. and Kolltveit, K. (2019) 'Why do civil servants experience media-stress differently and what can be done about it?', *Policy & Politics*, 47(4), pp. 599–620. https://doi.org/10.1332/030557319X15613701092525.

Schillemans, T., Overman, S., Fawcett, P. et al. (2021a) 'Conflictual accountability: Behavioral responses to conflictual accountability of agencies', *Administration & Society*, 53(8), pp. 1232–62. https://doi.org/10.1177/00953997211004606.

Schillemans, T., Overman, S., Fawcett, P. et al. (2021b) 'Understanding felt accountability', *Governance*, 34(3), pp. 893–916. https://doi.org/10.1111/gove.12547.

Schmidt, V. A. (2020) *Europe's Crisis of Legitimacy: Governing by Rules and Ruling by Numbers in the Eurozone*. Oxford: Oxford University Press.

Schonhardt-Bailey, C. (2022) *Deliberative Accountability in Parliamentary Committees*. Oxford: Oxford University Press.

Shaffer, G., Ginsburg, T. and Halliday, T. C. (eds.) (2019) *Constitution-Making and Transnational Legal Order*. Cambridge: Cambridge University Press.

Skelcher, C. and Smith, S. R. (2015) 'Theorizing hybridity: Institutional logics, complex organizations, and actor identities: The case of nonprofits', *Public Administration*, 93(2), pp. 433–48. https://doi.org/10.1111/padm.12105.

Sørensen, E. (2020) *Interactive Political Leadership: The Role of Politicians in the Age of Governance*. Oxford: Oxford University Press.

Sørensen, E., Hendriks, C. M., Hertting, N. and Edelenbos, J. (2020) 'Political boundary spanning: Politicians at the interface between collaborative governance and representative democracy', *Policy and Society*, 39(4), pp. 530–69. https://doi.org/10.1080/14494035.2020.1743526.

Sørensen, E. and Torfing, J. (2021) 'Accountable government through collaborative governance?', *Administrative Sciences*, 11(4), p. 127. https://doi.org/10.3390/admsci11040127.

Soroka, S. N. (2014) *Negativity in Democratic Politics: Causes and Consequences*. Cambridge: Cambridge University Press.

Soroka, S. N. and Wlezien, C. (2010) *Degrees of Democracy: Politics, Public Opinion, and Policy*. Cambridge: Cambridge University Press.

Stark, A. (2011) 'The tradition of ministerial responsibility and its role in the bureaucratic management of crises', *Public Administration*, 89(3), pp. 1148–63. https://doi.org/10.1111/j.1467-9299.2011.01924.x.

Stark, A. (2018) *Public Inquiries, Policy Learning, and the Threat of Future Crises*. Oxford: Oxford University Press.

Stimson, J. A., Mackuen, M. B. and Erikson, R. S. (1995) 'Dynamic representation', *The American Political Science Review*, 89(3), pp. 543–65. https://doi.org/10.2307/2082973.

Stokes, S. (2018) 'Accountability for realists', *Critical Review*, 30(1–2), pp. 130–8. https://doi.org/10.1080/08913811.2018.1473111.

Strom, K. (2000) 'Delegation and accountability in parliamentary democracies', *European Journal of Political Research*, 37(3), pp. 261–89. https://doi.org/10.1111/1475-6765.00513.

Svallfors, S. (2020) *Politics for Hire*. Cheltenham: Edward Elgar

Tetlock, P. E. (1991) 'An alternative metaphor in the study of judgment and choice: People as politicians', *Theory & Psychology*, 1(4), pp. 451–75. https://doi.org/10.1177/0959354391014004.

Tetlock, P. E. (1992) 'The impact of accountability on judgment and choice: Toward a social contingency model', *Advances in Experimental Social Psychology*, 25, pp. 331–76. https://doi.org/10.1016/S0065-2601(08)60287-7.

Tetlock, P. E. and Lerner, J. S. (1999) 'The social contingency model: Identifying empirical and normative boundary conditions on the error-and-bias portrait of human nature', in Chaiken, S. and Trope, Y. (eds.) *Dual-Process Theories in Social Psychology*. New York: Guilford Press, pp. 571–85.

Tetlock, P. E. and Manstead, A. S. (1985) 'Impression management versus intrapsychic explanations in social psychology: A useful dichotomy?', *Psychological Review*, 92(1), pp. 59–77. https://doi.org/10.1037/0033-295X.92.1.59.

Thomann, E., Hupe, P. and Sager, F. (2018) 'Serving many masters: Public accountability in private policy implementation', *Governance*, 31(2), pp. 299–319. https://doi.org/10.1111/gove.12297.

Thompson, D. F. (1980) 'Moral responsibility of public officials: The problem of many hands', *The American Political Science Review*, 74(4), pp. 905–16. https://doi.org/10.2307/1954312.

Tidå, B. (2022) 'Seeking the spotlight: How reputational considerations shape the European Court of Auditor's shifting account-holding role', *Public Administration*, 100(3), pp. 692–710. https://doi.org/10.1111/padm.12766.

Tilley, J. and Hobolt, S. B. (2011) 'Is the government to blame? An experimental test of how partisanship shapes perceptions of performance and responsibility', *The Journal of Politics*, 73(2), pp. 316–30. https://doi.org/10.1017/S0022381611000168.

Torfing, J., Sørensen, E. and Fotel, T. (2009) 'Democratic anchorage of infrastructural governance networks: The case of the Femern Belt Forum', *Planning Theory*, 8(3), pp. 282–308. https://doi.org/10.1177/1473095209104827.

Triantafillou, P. and Hansen, M. P. (2022) 'Introduction to the PMR special issue on accountability and legitimacy under collaborative governance', *Public Management Review*, 24(5), pp. 655–63. https://doi.org/10.1080/14719037.2021.2000744.

Tsebelis, G. (2003) *Veto Players: How Political Institutions Work*. Princeton: Princeton University Press.

Tu, W. and Gong, T. (2022) 'Accountability intensity and bureaucrats' response to conflicting expectations: A survey experiment in China', *Public Management Review*, 24(11), pp. 1779–801. https://doi.org/10.1080/14719037.2021.1930123.

Tucker, P. (2018) *Unelected Power: The Quest for Legitimacy in Central Banking and the Regulatory State*. Princeton: Princeton University Press.

Urbinati, N. and Warren, M. E. (2008) 'The concept of representation in contemporary democratic theory', *Annual Review of Political Science*, 11, pp. 387–412.

Vanberg, G. (2015) 'Constitutional courts in comparative perspective: A theoretical assessment', *Annual Review of Political Science*, 18(1), pp. 167–85. https://doi.org/10.1146/annurev-polisci-040113-161150.

Vandamme, P.-E. (2018) 'Voting secrecy and the right to justification', *Constellations*, 25(3), pp. 388–405. https://doi.org/10.1111/1467-8675.12278.

Vanhommerig, I. and Karré, P. M. (2014) 'Public accountability in the Internet age: Changing roles for governments and citizens', *International Review of Public Administration*, 19(2), pp. 206–17. https://doi.org/10.1080/12294659.2014.928477.

Verhoest, K., Roness, P., Verschuere, B., Rubecksen, K. and MacCarthaigh, M. (2010) *Autonomy and Control of State Agencies: Comparing States and Agencies*. London: Palgrave Macmillan.

Vibert, F. (2007) *The Rise of the Unelected: Democracy and the New Separation of Powers*. Cambridge: Cambridge University Press.

Vis, B. (2016) 'Taking stock of the comparative literature on the role of blame avoidance strategies in social policy reform', *Journal of Comparative Policy*

Analysis: Research and Practice, 18(2), pp. 122–37. https://doi.org/10.1080/13876988.2015.1005955.

Visram, S., Hunter, D. J., Perkins, N. et al. (2021) 'Health and wellbeing boards as theatres of accountability: A dramaturgical analysis', *Local Government Studies*, 47(6), pp. 931–50. https://doi.org/10.1080/03003930.2020.1816543.

de Vries, C. E. and Giger, N. (2014) 'Holding governments accountable? Individual heterogeneity in performance voting', *European Journal of Political Research*, 53(2), pp. 345–62. https://doi.org/10.1111/1475-6765.12033.

de Vries, C. E. and Solaz, H. (2017) 'The electoral consequences of corruption', *Annual Review of Political Science*, 20(1), pp. 391–408. https://doi.org/10.1146/annurev-polisci-052715-111917.

Waldron, J. (2014) *Accountability: Fundamental to Democracy*. NYU School of Law, Public Law Research Paper No. 14–13. https://doi.org/10.2139/ssrn.2410812.

Weaver, R. K. (1986) 'The politics of blame avoidance', *Journal of Public Policy*, 6(4), pp. 371–98.

de Wilde, P. and Rauh, C. (2019) 'Going full circle: The need for procedural perspectives on EU responsiveness', *Journal of European Public Policy*, 26(11), pp.1737–48. https://doi.org/10.1080/13501763.2019.1668043.

Willems, T. and Van Dooren, W. (2012) 'Coming to terms with accountability', *Public Management Review*, 14(7), pp. 1011–36. https://doi.org/10.1080/14719037.2012.662446.

Willems, T. and Van Dooren, W. (2017) 'Multiple accountabilities in public-private partnerships (PPs): How to unravel the accountability paradox?', in Christensen, T. and Lægreid, P. (eds.) *The Routledge Handbook to Accountability and Welfare State Reforms in Europe*. Abingdon: Routledge, pp. 255–66.

Wood, M., Matthews, F., Overman, S. and Schillemans, T. (2022) 'Enacting accountability under populist pressures: Theorizing the relationship between anti-elite rhetoric and public accountability', *Administration & Society*, 54(2), pp. 311–34. https://doi.org/10.1177/00953997211019387.

Wright, T. (2015) 'The politics of accountability', in Feldman, D. and Elliott, M. (eds.) *The Cambridge Companion to Public Law*. Cambridge: Cambridge University Press, pp. 96–115.

Wu, S. and Christensen, T. (2021) 'Corruption and accountability in China's rural poverty governance: Main features from village and township cadres', *International Journal of Public Administration*, 44(16), pp. 1383–93. https://doi.org/10.1080/01900692.2020.1765799.

Yang, K. (2012) 'Further understanding accountability in public organizations: Actionable knowledge and the structure–agency duality', *Administration & Society*, 44(3), pp. 255–84. https://doi.org/10.1177/0095399711417699.

Yeung, K. and Lodge, M. (eds.) (2019) *Algorithmic Regulation*. Oxford: Oxford University Press.

Acknowledgements

While writing this Element, I had the privilege to count on the constant intellectual and emotional support of Sandrine. This Element is dedicated to her and to my children Alba, Floria, Amalia and Victor, who remind me of the importance of life outside work and of accountability within the family. This Element has been published open access with the support of the Swiss National Science Foundation. I would like to thank the Institut d'Etudes Politiques of the University of Lausanne for covering part of my English editing costs. I am very grateful to Peter Hupe and Jacint Jordana for their careful reading of the draft manuscript and their insightful comments, to the two anonymous reviewers who provided high-quality reviews and valuable recommendations and to the editors of the Elements in Public Policy series for their patience and helpful guidance. Any errors or misinterpretations that remain are my sole responsibility.

Cambridge Elements ≡

Public Policy

M. Ramesh
National University of Singapore (NUS)

M. Ramesh is UNESCO Chair on Social Policy Design at the Lee Kuan Yew School of Public Policy, NUS. His research focuses on governance and social policy in East and Southeast Asia, in addition to public policy institutions and processes. He has published extensively in reputed international journals. He is Co-editor of Policy and Society and Policy Design and Practice.

Michael Howlett
Simon Fraser University, British Columbia

Michael Howlett is Burnaby Mountain Professor and Canada Research Chair (Tier 1) in the Department of Political Science, Simon Fraser University. He specialises in public policy analysis, and resource and environmental policy. He is currently editor-in-chief of *Policy Sciences* and co-editor of the *Journal of Comparative Policy Analysis, Policy and Society and Policy Design and Practice*.

Xun WU
Hong Kong University of Science and Technology

Xun WU is Professor and Head of the Division of Public Policy at the Hong Kong University of Science and Technology. He is a policy scientist whose research interests include policy innovations, water resource management and health policy reform. He has been involved extensively in consultancy and executive education, his work involving consultations for the World Bank and UNEP.

Judith Clifton
University of Cantabria

Judith Clifton is Professor of Economics at the University of Cantabria, Spain. She has published in leading policy journals and is editor-in-chief of the *Journal of Economic Policy Reform*. Most recently, her research enquires how emerging technologies can transform public administration, a forward-looking cutting-edge project which received €3.5 million funding from the Horizon2020 programme.

Eduardo Araral
National University of Singapore (NUS)

Eduardo Araral is widely published in various journals and books and has presented in forty conferences. He is currently Co-Director of the Institute of Water Policy at the Lee Kuan Yew School of Public Policy, NUS, and is a member of the editorial board of *Journal of Public Administration Research and Theory* and the board of the Public Management Research Association.

About the Series
Elements in Public Policy is a concise and authoritative collection of assessments of the state of the art and future research directions in public policy research, as well as substantive new research on key topics. Edited by leading scholars in the field, the series is an ideal medium for reflecting on and advancing the understanding of critical issues in the public sphere. Collectively, the series provides a forum for broad and diverse coverage of all major topics in the field while integrating different disciplinary and methodological approaches.

Cambridge Elements ☰

Public Policy

Elements in the Series

How Ideas and Institutions Shape the Politics of Public Policy
Daniel Béland

Policy Entrepreneurs and Dynamic Change
Michael Mintrom

Making Global Policy
Diane Stone

Understanding and Analyzing Public Policy Design
Saba Siddiki

Zombie Ideas: Why Failed Policy Ideas Persist
Brainard Guy Peters and Maximilian Lennart Nagel

Defining Policy Analysis: A Journey that Never Ends
Beryl A. Radin

Integrating Logics in the Governance of Emerging Technologies: The Case of Nanotechnology
Derrick Mason Anderson and Andrew Whitford

Truth and Post-Truth in Public Policy
Frank Fischer

Disrupted Governance: Towards a New Policy Science
Kris Hartley Glen David Kuecker

Digital Technology, Politics, and Policy-Making
Fabrizio Gilardi

Public Policy and Universities: The Interplay of Knowledge and Power
Andrew Gunn and Michael Mintrom

Understanding Accountability in Democratic Governance
Yannis Papadopoulos

A full series listing is available at: www.cambridge.org/EPPO

·

Printed in the United States
by Baker & Taylor Publisher Services